Other Shores

Other Shores

DIANA NYAD

 RANDOM HOUSE NEW YORK

Portions of this book originally appeared in the May/
June issue of Quest/78 and in the April 1978 issue
of Mademoiselle.

Library of Congress Cataloging in Publication Data

Nyad, Diana.
Other shores.
Bibliography: p.
1. Nyad, Diana. 2. Swimmers—Biography. i. Title.
GV838.N9A34   797.2'1'0924   78-56910
ISBN 0-394-50175-6

Manufactured in the United States of America
9 8 7 6 5 4 3 2
First Edition

for my mother,
my first hero

Acknowledgments

I would like to acknowledge the help I received from Conrad Wennerberg's book Wind, Waves and Sunburn, *which is the only thorough, accurate and loving treatise on marathon swimming available. His factual research has often set me straight, and his anecdotes have entertained me for months.*

Second, my thanks to the writers in the Frederick Lewis Allen Room at the New York Public Library. They became friends who were never too busy to take an interest in a fledgling young writer. Also one friend, Candace Lyle Hogan, helped me throughout with her comments and encouragement.

Author's Note

After a six-month writing stretch, I sat down with the completed manuscript of this book to see exactly what I had created. However delighted I was with some aspects of it, I was appalled to discover that the persona of the book, myself, came across as such an overly dramatic braggart. I tried to tone the drama down here and there, but it seems I am simply not given to understatement. My world view is dramatic. Every minute seems like the most important minute of my life. I don't expect the reader to identify with my extremity; I only ask him to accept it.

I should also ask acceptance of my arrogance. I pride myself on the fact that I respect others and listen to others and that I know the value of every individual's life is precisely equal to my own. I was surprised to find, as I read my own book, what a high opinion of myself I harbor. It will perhaps be offensive to some. My rationale is that this book is my home turf; self-esteem is only natural.

Contents

Other Shores

I. Lake Ontario

〜〜〜〜〜〜〜〜〜〜〜〜〜〜〜〜〜〜〜〜〜〜〜〜〜〜〜〜〜〜〜〜〜〜

"EIGHT THOUSAND four hundred. Should I ask the time? No, I know the time. Five hours, thirty-six minutes. Six hundred strokes to go; twenty-four minutes. Hang on, stay strong. Finish strong. Four hundred one, two, three . . ."

I was finishing the last training swim in June 1974. Fifteen miles in Lake Ontario. My trainer, Cliff Lumsdon, the best marathon swimmer in the world in the early fifties, was cruising next to me in the motorized inflatable, *Rubber Ducky*. He steered the course, kept me away from debris and boats, and clocked my miles as we reached the markers. But I didn't need to be told how fast I was going or how far I had gone. I set a rhythmic, balanced pace of 2.5 m.p.h. and never wavered. Six hundred strokes to the mile, every mile in twenty-four minutes. Fifteen miles in six hours. Nine thousand strokes.

I glided one stroke past the last marker, floated on my back for thirty seconds, then pulled my goggles up onto my forehead with a sigh and a smile. Cliff pulled me into *Rub-*

ber Ducky and wrapped me in towels, and we putted back home, grinning all the way. The work was over. Miles and miles of slow distance, September through December. The races in South America, January and February. Sprints and interval work in the pool, March and April. Outdoor training with Cliff, May and June. Hours every day. Thoroughly exhausted every day. Bored with the repetition, fed up with the inflexible eat, sleep, swim routine. This fifteen-miler marked the welcome end of many trying months. The following day I was leaving for Italy. There was to be a race across the Bay of Naples, and I was ready.

Cliff's apartment looks over Lake Ontario. We could see Cliff's windows from miles away; finally we approached and pulled *Rubber Ducky* up over the rocks. While Cliff took care of the boat and gear, I went up to settle in a steamy bath. The lake had been 61 degrees, so I was chilled and liable to become stiff.

On my way upstairs I mentally searched once again for a brainstorm and a plane ticket for Cliff. The marathon-swim organizers weren't poor—just cheap. Here I was, in one of the most difficult sports in the world where you work your heart out for too many hours, sometimes freezing or vomiting, always uncomfortable. Couldn't possibly make a living, but it was great food for pride. Like boxing in the fifties. If you weren't a primo heavyweight, you trained your guts out in a less-than-adequate gym in Brooklyn. You took the bus to Kansas City, made $50 if you won, spent $35 to cover the gash over your eye and a trainer's percent, and tried to make it back to the gym in Brooklyn to get ready for the next one. I spent $800, saved from my last swim, on my own plane fare to Rome. The first-place prize for this one would be $650, so I had lost on that count before the race began.

INTO THE TUB. The tepid water comforts me, seduces me, and the daydream begins. I talk to pinpoints on the tiles, imaginary faces. Explaining how I mustered the courage, how I maintained the discipline, why I set out to conquer such difficult mountains. I finish my speech, the fantasy fades; I towel-dry and join Cliff on the balcony.

HOOKED ARM IN ARM, sipping hot chocolate, we gazed out at the sunset over the lake. Cliff said he hoped I would win the Italy race; I told him he could count on it. Dinner, a massage, and a sound night's sleep. I slept in until 7:00 and looked forward to an unusual day of relaxation. My plane was scheduled for 4:30; Cliff went to work, said he would pick me up at 2:45. I packed, ate, read, and at noon decided to go down for a loose preflight swim. The sun was hot; kids were playing up and down the bluff. I asked a man if he would watch my towel and sneakers for an hour. He said, "You're not going in the lake, are you?" I smiled and strutted to the water's edge. In this sport, you recognize backhanded compliments when you hear them. The water washed up over my feet; I caught my breath and jumped back. "Come on, Nyad. You just want to get on that plane. This hour will do you good, help you meditate, finalize your thoughts. Get in there!"

I dived in and my heart stopped. Depending on the change in wind direction, Lake Ontario can make an extreme about-face in temperature of up to 20 degrees within twenty-four hours. And this, I knew, was no 61 degrees. Far from it. The work was supposed to be over; I shouldn't have to put myself through another utterly unnecessary hour of discomfort. On the other hand, I thought I was exaggerating the cold. Thought I was pampering. I would go a thousand strokes straight out and a thousand back. One hour, eight minutes.

A thousand strokes usually takes me just over a mile and a half. I stopped at the count and realized I had barely moved. My arms had been spinning to generate warmth. My legs were immobile and folded up under my chest. For a painful five minutes, I maneuvered my body around to face the shore. Only then did I discover that I had traveled a mere four hundred yards. I was scared. My jaw was open and locked; throat rigid and unable to scream; fingers spread and useless. I began a slow, inefficient breast stroke and in half an hour made half the distance. Two hundred lousy yards, but I was paralyzed. Barely keeping myself afloat, bobbing lower and lower, I was hit by the full irony of the very definite possibility that I was about to drown. Another attempt at a scream, but all my breath seemed to be caught in my mouth and no sound would come. Some signal must have traveled, however, because I could then see the kids running up and down the shore, waving their arms frantically at me, yelling for help. Hope renews strength; I was floundering forward again. I had made it forty yards from shore when I noticed a man in khaki pants and sneakers, bounding over the bluff. As I reached the half-submerged rocks, he splashed into the water and was to me within thirty seconds. From behind he threw his arms over my shoulders, hooking his hands in my armpits, and hefted me onto a sunbaked rock. I was shivering uncontrollably, moaning sounds instead of words, and by the time the ambulance came I realized that the warmth of this man's hands had burned the front of my shoulders. His 98.6-degree hands had left two bloody wounds. What could the water temperature have been?

I was warmed in a body oven and had my shoulder wounds dressed. The doctor called the Coast Guard for me. The lake was 40 degrees. Forty degrees! I had nearly drowned, I had missed the plane to Rome, but all I could think of was beating Lake Ontario. I felt like a boxer who had been given a sting that couldn't be forgotten and who couldn't wait to climb back into the ring. I wanted Lake Ontario. Five people had crossed her south to north. No mean feat. Thirty-two miles across a cold, wavy and very fickle Great Lake. But there was some assistance from the strong Niagara River currents, which shoot out with the swimmer from the southern shore for about five miles until they are dissipated. Always looking for the near-impossible dream, I asked Cliff if anyone had ever swum it north to south. He shook his head, said it would be tricky fighting the currents after making it most of the way across; you couldn't afford to be weakened at that point. I pronounced that I wanted to make a double crossing: over the hard way, north to south, and back the "easy" way. Cliff laughed out loud, but when our eyes met, the silent handshake was made to go after Lake Ontario together.

I was late to Italy, the burns were slow to heal, but the race went in my favor anyway. I broke the world's record. Eight hours, eleven minutes, across the Bay of Naples. I recuperated, got my weight and strength back, and was off to five more races, one each weekend. The fifth one was on a Sunday, twenty-five miles across a cold lake in northern Quebec. I was supposed to be in Chicago for the Lake Michigan race by Thursday; and after that there would be an ocean swim down the west coast of Mexico.

I never showed up in Chicago. Nor in Mexico. It was a difficult decision, because the races meant money, however little, as well as points for world standing. But it was the second week of August and I knew Lake Ontario could not be had come September. So Cliff and I were back in the Toronto apartment, planning the incredible two-way crossing that six weeks earlier had been nothing more than a fantasy, a laugh and a handshake. You couldn't see the rugs for the charts; counters and tables were cluttered with thermoses, grease jars and glucose bottles; bathing suits hung from every doorknob; and the phone rang every minute of the day.

Toronto is a city with a history of enthusiasm for long-distance swimming. Fifty thousand fans had annually lined the shore of Lake Ontario to watch Cliff and swimmers from all over the world battle for the Canadian National Exhibition prize money during unending hours in the bitterly cold water for which the lake had gained its reputation. Since Toronto natives know all the great swimmers by name and nationality and can quote you most of their records, stirring up some public interest for this swim was not a difficult task. First of all, Big Cliff was a national sports hero and I was his swimmer. Second, I was running off at the mouth about double crossing the lake they knew so well and duly feared. Only five of the best swimmers to date had made it south to north; they had too much respect for the awesome body of water to imagine that anyone could go it the other way, against the Niagara River currents. And they guffawed at the outright lunacy of going over and back again. Every television and radio station, every newspaper and magazine in Toronto did a story on the loony but refreshing New Yorker about to embark on her pointless journey.

An old friend of Cliff's agreed to help us with the charts for currents and the navigation on the day of the swim. With radar equipment, he would proceed one hundred yards ahead of us, constantly changing the course according to cross or head winds and my ability to fight them. The navigator's vessel is especially helpful at night as we simply follow the green light at the top of his mast. But I still had to spend an afternoon at the boat basin looking for an adventurer. A couple finally volunteered their forty-foot yacht as escort boat—the boat that always stays on my right by about thirty yards, carrying equipment and serving as resting boat for the crew. *Rubber Ducky* is on my immediate left so that when I lift my face to breathe, although I don't have time to focus fully, I can swim in a straight line by checking my constant distance from the boat. If the crew need to relay some information to me, they blow a police whistle and I hesitate during the breath in order to read the huge blackboard. Also, I need to receive a glucose supplement every hour, and *Rubber Ducky* is ideal for feeding: its rubberized pontoons enable me to come very close to take the cup of hot glucose with relative safety.

Cliff, as chief trainer, would be next to me all the time, boarding the yacht for relief every three or four hours. Cliff's daughter would be pacer, coming in to swim with me for a half-hour every five or six hours when I reached the desperate low points. Two of the Lake Ontario frogmen would be running *Rubber Ducky,* prepared for emergencies or repairs. And my four best buddies would be there to help Cliff and to lend much-appreciated moral support. The rest was up to me.

Mid-August is always the point in the season when I am my absolute strongest. And that year was no exception: I had just trained like a bandit for nine months, competed in six very tough races and rested for a full week. If anybody could make this swim, I could. The weather was right on the 16th, so we set the starting time for 7:00 A.M.

Up at 4:30. Six raw eggs, cereal, toast with honey, hot protein liquid with glucose. Fill the thermoses, double-check the supplies, run through the signals. I am pensive the morning of a swim; I know too well what lies in store for me. The crew is loading the boats by 6:00. I pose, joke, philosophize for the press. Trainers begin greasing my body at 6:50. Everyone shouts their best-of-luck phrases; I make a final adjustment of the goggles and the four bathing caps I wear for warmth. I take the plunge.

It is a beautiful, clear day. Water temperature, 72 degrees. Outside the harbor, the lake is almost smooth. For the first three hours, I make incredible progress. Stroking strongly, sixty strokes to the minute, doing counting tricks in my head to pass the time, stopping for ten seconds every hour on the hour to down the glucose drink. A head wind comes up during the fourth hour. A two-foot chop. This wind increases steadily during the next six hours, so that by the tenth hour I am fighting six- and seven-footers. My arms are weakened from slapping and punching walls of water on every stroke. And now I am shivering with the cold. The water temperature has dropped to 63 degrees. The grease has for the most part washed off, and I realize I'm not even close to the other shore. I will not, however, let doubt take its turn in my mind. A pacer would be helpful at this point, but I decide to wait for the return trip. I can't afford to worry about getting over, because on a double crossing, getting back is obviously the difficulty. Fear comes quickly on the heels of self-doubt. Fear that I am not worthy of the goal, that the commitment has been too heavy, that I have risked showing myself a quitter by chasing such an unreasonable dream. This is the first sign that intense concentration and mental control will be needed for every coming minute.

AT THIS POINT I had swum literally thousands of miles during my long-distance career. I had crossed lakes, rivers and seas all around the world. And the battle against fear, doubt and boredom had long ago become a major one. The human mind is not geared to focus on any concrete consideration such as money or victory or position for many minutes at a time. Therefore, even during a short period such as an hour, when the mind is thoroughly isolated, it begins to wander, to abstract. And twelve, twenty or thirty hours of continual stress through a monotonous, almost intuitive exercise can become the greatest test of concentration—especially allowing for the fact that not only is the swimmer usually delirious or semi-delirious from fatigue but he is also disoriented from the hours of sensory deprivation.

Dark goggles cover the eyes; the head turns some sixty times a minute toward the boat so that eye focus is almost never achieved. Tight rubber caps inhibit hearing to the point that a shrill police whistle often can't be heard from a twenty-foot distance. Both tactile sense and balance are seriously distorted so that your body feels only an uncontrolled, floaty sensation. In short, for thirty hours you are left with nothing at all but your own thoughts. You must concentrate on keeping your will strong enough to resist the various bombarding pains while occupying your mind with something other than the pain itself. After a very few hours into a difficult swim, your thoughts begin to drift. The danger comes when you drift so far that you lose touch with what you're doing. Then it is impossible to continue, to watch the boat every stroke, to come in for the feedings, to remember why you are going through this agony.

Once toward the end of a quick-paced race in Argentina,

I stopped excitedly, turned toward my trainer in a panic and told her that the Catholics were on the shore. She was experienced in the delirium and the euphoria of long-distance swimmers; she told me that I should keep swimming and she'd take care of the Catholics. As far as I know, I have never felt one way or the other about Catholics—my mind had drifted so far that I had lost all conscious control.

And once in an ocean swim one of my Australian friends saw a huge barbed-wire fence on her right. She screamed frantically to the boat crew that they were pushing her into the fence, which was about to cut her skin. They knew it was foolish to attempt to bring her back to reality; instead, they came to her fantasy. They pretended concern, veered to the left away from the imaginary fence, and agreed with her during the next feeding that it was indeed a dangerously close call. These consuming fantasies are amusing in retrospect, but at the time they are significant warning signals. Swimmers have been known to drift so far that they begin swimming in tiny circles, unable to regain the concentration needed to proceed toward the finish line.

After the first few years on the pro circuit, I decided to devise a mental program to remain better in touch as the hours passed. My steady, balanced stroke lends itself to counting numbers for distance traveled: if six hundred strokes make a mile, eighteen hundred strokes make three miles. And if singing "Row, Row, Row Your Boat" completes eight strokes, then seventy-five "Row, Row, Row Your Boat"s make a mile. I found that making simple counting goals for each hour kept me close enough to total concentration that I could proceed indefinitely at a good pace, while also letting me escape far enough that the discomfort and the boredom were not overbearing. With this hypnotic technique I know precisely what I am doing, yet I can give in to extreme fantasy and sleeplike dreaming. Colors become vivid, unexpected scenes and images flash before my eyes, sexual images are particularly strong. I am dreaming, yet performing extraordinary feats. I used this counting technique in Lake Ontario.

THE GOAL of the fifteenth hour: seventy-five "Frère Jacques"s. Shortly after the fifteenth feeding I catch a glimpse of lights from the shore. It is 10:00 P.M. I ask Cliff and he affirms; we are getting there. As they say, however, we must take the bad with the good. The currents from the Niagara River are reaching to push me away and they become more and more effective as we approach the shore. I am shaking uncontrollably, frustrated by the fact that the currents push me one stroke back for every two I take forward. I don't complain; I don't speak at all. Head down, arms weak but steady—very determined.

At 1:20 A.M. I touch the shore after 18 hours and 20 minutes of nonstop swimming. I am frozen, my legs can't support me, my arms feel bruised from battling the waves for so many hours, and even though I am psyching up for the return trip which must begin in ten minutes (all official double crossings in marathon swimming allow no more than ten minutes on the other shore), I allow myself a moment of glory. I know that I am the first and only person, male or female, to have crossed this brutal beast north to south. The press zero in, trying to get close enough to catch a glimpse of the young woman who just made a reality of what was supposed lunacy.

The police rope off a small square on the beach, like a boxer's ring. The crew sit me in a chair, regrease me, feed me some solid food, change my caps, and post me on the time every thirty seconds. Cliff knows better than anyone that I am utterly exhausted; I have lost a great deal of weight and strength. He whispers softly in my ear: "You just completed a great swim; you don't have to get back in there if you don't want to." But I have to try. I walk back into the water at 1:30 A.M.; I am chilled to the bone but I start stroking, and after an hour or so, I feel better. During a breath I yell that I'm going to make it. Cliff gives me the thumbs-up sign. All my friends cheer from the yacht, and the flotilla of boats that has accompanied us through the night blare their horns. At 20 hours, 30 minutes, I lose consciousness.

IN MY HEART, the Lake Ontario swim was a success. A grand success. Against near-impossible odds, I made it to the southern shore and had the courage to walk back into that frozen dark for the return trip. That's what those people who wait on shorelines admire—the courage. They don't care if a group of eighty are racing for prize money from Capri to Naples or if one young woman is trying to conquer Lake Ontario the hard way for her pride. They don't care if the swimmer breaks a world record or finishes twenty hours slower than expected. They gather by the thousands on the shores of Argentinean rivers, Australian oceans and Canadian lakes to stare at an individual who has pushed herself beyond every conceivable limit. They are fascinated by this thoroughly spent body, this 110 percent effort, especially in an era when motivation is deteriorating and limitations are rarely pushed. They are willing to wait long hours for one quick glimpse of a most extreme moment. Sometimes I walk out of a swim on my own, often I need help, and occasionally I go by on the ambulance stretcher. They are always there. The men yell "Bravo, Diana!" "Fantastic!" "Brave young woman!" And the women just stare. Incredulous, awe-filled, envious stares. The utter exhaustion, and the courage it conveys, seems to be an inspiration to everyone who witnesses it.

2. The Pro Circuit

I SUPPOSE IT BEGAN when my parents moved to Fort Lauderdale, Florida. I was thrown into the middle of the pool at six months and swam to the edge. By the time I was old enough to learn what a Nyad was (nai.ad 1. in Greek and Roman mythology, any of the nymphs who lived in and gave life to springs, fountains, rivers and lakes. 2. a girl or woman swimmer), destiny had taken its course and I was to be found cavorting in the surf during every waking hour.

When I was eleven years old and in the seventh grade, the geography teacher said that anyone who came out for the junior high swimming team would get an A in geography. This kind of bribery appealed to me, so I showed up, suit in hand, on the pool deck that afternoon. The coach, Jack Nelson, who had already coached several young women to national titles, later became the coach of the women's Olympic team in Montreal, 1976. He helped me to improve enough within that first year to become the best in the state of Florida at both the 100-meter and 200-meter backstroke.

Nelson explained to me that I had two assets common to all world-class swimmers. First, I had the genetic ability, a feel for the water and the perfect physique for a swimmer—a slender body with a relatively high center of gravity, enormous strength in the upper body and very little weight in the hips and legs. And second, I had the psychological hunger to put myself through pain when the goal warranted it. As it turned out, Nelson was right.

From age eleven to age sixteen I lived a spartan life without the usual adolescent uncertainty. I wanted to be the best swimmer in the world, and there was nothing else. Schoolwork was easy for me. Friendships were also easy for me. Top-flight swimmers from all over the country were sent down to our school to swim with Nelson. This extremely talented group of young women shared both an obsession about the work we were performing and a mature seriousness about pursuing our goals. I made lifetime buddies during those years. These were friendships cultivated through the sharing of disciplines; I had no interest in other social interaction.

I was up at 4:30, 5:00 or 5:30 (depending on the time of year) every day of the year, including Christmas. The routine was a two-hour workout, classes until lunch break, an hour of sprints, school until 4:00 and another two-hour workout after school. Summers were more vigorous. I would be so tired at night I couldn't eat dinner. My sister would bring me something in bed. And often my eyes would be swollen shut from the hours of immersion in the heavily chlorinated water (the small plastic goggles weren't around at that time). My mother used to make ice packs for my eyes, and once she could ease them open a bit, she would squirt drops in them and bathe them in cold water. I remem-

ber the pain in my eyes as if it were yesterday. Coach Nelson
has subsequently told interviewers that I was the hardest
worker he'd ever had. I would stop after a repeat, throw my
guts up in the gutter and push off again for the next one.
I wasn't afraid to dig down for everything I had. And the
hard work paid off. At sixteen I was not the very best in the
world, but I was damn good.

One day in June 1966, the summer after junior year, I had
a scare of bad chest pains while training, and the EKG
turned up a severe case of viral endocarditis. The cardiolo-
gist's theory was that when I had contracted a severe cold
and accompanying fever, I continued to train heavily for
several weeks and the cold virus eventually moved to the
center of activity, the heart. Viral endocarditis surrounds
the heart and can't be treated by antibiotics or anything
other than rest. I spent three months in strict bed rest. I read
all day, with intermittent conversations with my sister—who
spent every minute of every day with me—my brother, and
my mother. When two months had passed, I spent another
month in more moderate bed rest, but still not going out of
the house, much less exercising. I had become so weak and
had lost so much weight during those three months that it
was a full year until I was my strong self again. That senior
year was a frustrating disappointment. I tried like hell and
Coach Nelson and the kids were all behind me, but I just
wasn't strong enough. Any outside hope for the 1968 Olympic games was crushed; it was time for college where women
at that time had neither scholarships nor adequate coaching,
so I bid swimming a sad adieu.

First year of college was Emory University in Atlanta,
Georgia—the worst year of my life. Skipping a thorough
psychological analysis, I will simply say that this was my

belated, confused, adolescent year. Following a very long sequence of nightmares (not least of which was my jumping from the fourth-story window with an opened parachute— a *Sports Illustrated* mention—in a desperately crude, immature and exhibitionistic cry for attention), I was kicked out of Emory. The dean of women gravely touched her framed Phi Beta Kappa certificate, saying that such an honor was bestowed upon superior students and superior persons— which is why I would never be eligible. She suggested intensive psychological care and told me to pack up. I went back to Fort Lauderdale to make some money of my own and to see a shrink so that I could prove my sanity and get into school somewhere. I was a recluse; I wouldn't talk to anyone but my mother; I spent every hour of the day alone, running long hours on the beach, reading and writing by the sea. I tried to get in everywhere: Berkeley, University of Michigan, Yale. Just as it seemed that no one was going to give me another chance (I felt like an ex-con), Lake Forest College in Lake Forest, Illinois, let me in. They called me December 27, 1970, and I was there for classes January 2. I felt I was about to emerge again after being down an awfully long time. Academics became incredibly exciting to me; I was Phi Beta Kappa in my junior year.

Midway through that first term at Lake Forest, Buck Dawson, an old friend, called with a tempting prospect of trying the marathon swimming circuit. As the director of the Swimming Hall of Fame in Fort Lauderdale, he had seen me grow up, seen the difficulties I'd had after the endocarditis, and was sensitive enough to know exactly what marathon swimming and I would do for each other. Buck is bald, has a great body for a twenty-five-year-old even though he's fifty-three, and wears a black patch over his left eye. Friends call him Moshe—or Captain Patch. He is an adventurer par excellence, has written twenty full-length novels and has never held a real nine-to-five job. He and his wife run a competitive swimming camp for girls in the north woods of Ontario, about four hours up from Toronto. Buck stands up there on the hilltops, cups his hands and booms, "Hero was a woman!" a sound that echoes for miles and miles.

In the mid-sixties Buck had taken one of Michigan's best amateur swimmers, Marty Sinn, and trained her for long pro-circuit swims in the lakes at his camp. She did very well for two years, beating a lot of the best men in the business. But she found the sport unnecessarily masochistic, so she quit way before her prime. Buck had been looking for another champion ever since. I must have seemed perfect: I had speed, which was not always the case among the marathoners; I had proven tremendous resistance to pain, which was the first requirement in this sport; and I was growling with hunger after "failing" at amateur swimming, so there would be a strong incentive to get across those lakes, rivers and oceans.

Toward the end of the 1970 school year I put in some distance in the Lake Forest pool, and from the middle of May to the middle of July I whipped myself into shape at Michigan State University with a very tough coach, Dick Fetters. I rented an apartment two blocks from the pool, stocked the refrigerator and buried myself. After laying off any tough interval work for more than two years, the first week was the most grueling training experience I can remember. I swam six hours a day in three sessions, and my only goal was to survive each session and attempt to recuperate in time to survive the next session. For a solid week, except for the actual time in the pool, I lay flat on my back with a definite Kafkaesque sensation of needles carving the word EXHAUSTION deeper and deeper into my muscles. I would barely drag myself back to the apartment, try to ease my stomach so I could eat and drink, and literally pass out until the alarm would signal time to hit the pool again. It seemed that I had let it go too long and that I would never get in shape again, but during the third week I felt an ounce of strength. And by the end of the fourth week it was glorious to be doing what I had once been a master at.

I went up to Buck's camp in Canada—paradise on earth. I had no idea what I was in for, but the newness of swimming freely for miles and miles in the cool, clean lakes was fantastic. I was reading all the legends of long-distance swimming and Buck, with his talent for histrionics, filled me in with the anecdotes from recent years. Long-distance running, long-distance swimming, and probably some form of hand-to-hand combat are the primeval sports that have existed in forms other than sport since before recorded history. It was the conquering of geographical space with the human body and will that defined survival; and it is precisely the simplistic and primitive nature of these activities that has kept them alive in literature and in the era of modern sport as well.

I learned that long-distance swims are recorded throughout the years as homage to that notion that man with his insignificant size and strength can occasionally affirm his place and his power in the universe by defying and conquering the elements. Even with the marvel of environmental control we have reached in this technological twentieth century, the attraction of marathon running and marathon swimming is stronger than ever. And the primary seduction is the idea that you defeat the elements and you overcome geographical space with no aid or equipment other than your own strength of body and spirit.

The primeval nature of the long-distance swim renders it a fascinating entity at any period in history. One of the oldest myths of swimming is that of Leander, who swam the forty miles of the Hellespont every night to meet with his lover, Hero. (The Hellespont—the Dardanelles—has become a popular swim for twentieth-century marathoners.) There was a long-standing theory that Charlemagne swam across the English Channel in the late eighth century, but we take as fact that the first crossing belonged to Captain Matthew Webb of England, who drank brandy for warmth and smeared his skin with porpoise oil. Byron was a famed swimmer, Ben Franklin was posthumously inducted into the International Swimming Hall of Fame, and Gertrude Ederle became a millionaire after she swam the English Channel in 1926, the first woman to do so.

I read hundreds of cases of men who have swum to save their lives after ships have gone under, submarines have been hit and planes have been ditched. The most frightening story is that of an Ecuadorian pilot and two crew members who were forced to come down in the Pacific off Salinas because of technical malfunction. They had secured life jackets before hitting the water. They began swimming toward what they guessed was shore but one of the crewmen was troubled by the high seas and swallowed a great deal of salt water. About five hours after the forced landing, he died. The pilot kept stroking toward shore, pushing his friend's corpse ahead of him. Some six hours after the crash, sharks circled the three men and slowly dismembered the dead man until they had eaten the entire body. The pilot and the remaining crewman were dreadfully frightened, but they kept moving forward. Shortly thereafter, the crewman reached a point of exhaustion beyond which he couldn't fend for himself. The pilot egged him on, but then he died, and the pilot again pushed a corpse along in front of him. It was the middle of the night; eerily lighted by the moonlight, the black shadows surfaced. The pilot silently watched his second friend disappear. He made it through the night and swam throughout the next day, all the while scared to death, as sharks would brush his legs if he let them dangle for a minute's rest. After thirty-one hours of swimming he thankfully stumbled onto shore and collapsed until some passers-by discovered him a few hours later. (Thirty-one hours in open sea water is considered a highly respectable swim for a marathoner who has a boat ten feet away and who can replenish his body fluids and sugars as much as need be.)

Another amazing survival story is that of a young Korean who fell overboard in the Pacific. It was night and his freighter was traveling at too high a speed to notice the splash. He had been swimming continuously for some twelve hours when he saw a dark form rising to the surface; he panicked, thinking it was a shark, but luckily a giant sea turtle popped up next to him. Sea biologists say that sea turtles would not befriend a human in the open Pacific, but this one seemed to sense the Korean's fate and gave him a free ride for more than three hours, at which time they were both spotted by a Swedish ship.

Even in the animal world, nothing can outdo an endurance feat for fascination, although the talents of great bursts of speed are always applauded. The cheetah must be glorified for his running speed of over sixty miles per hour, and the porpoise is highly commended for a swimming speed of over thirty knots. But the distances that animals have swum nonstop are simply outrageous. Polar bears have been sighted seventy-five miles from the nearest land; tigers have swum at least fourteen miles in the Java Sea to reach the islands around the Malay Peninsula; elephants have swum out twenty-five miles from the coast of East Africa, and the gold-medal winner is probably the Pacific salmon, which swims continuously for twelve or more days, day and night, without rest or food, to complete its life cycle.

I read all these inspirational tales up at Buck's paradise, swimming five and six hours in the lakes every day. And I learned just what the pro circuit was. In 1927, William Wrigley, Jr., of chewing-gum fame, offered $40,000 total prize money, $25,000 to the winner, in a race from Catalina Island to the California coast. It turned into a two-man battle between two-time Olympian Norman Ross of Chicago and a kid from Toronto, George Young. The Canadian won in 15 hours, 45 minutes and made the swim such a media success that Wrigley sponsored a series of professional swims in Lake Ontario that have never been matched since. The Canadian National Exhibition is an extravagant fair that takes place on the Toronto shore during the last two weeks of each August. On August 30, 1927, half a year after the first Catalina Island race, swimmers arrived from all around the world to compete for the $30,000 first-place prize. A twenty-one-mile circuit race in front of the C.N.E. grandstands, it was won by Ernst Vierkotter of Germany. More than 35,000 fans paid to witness the event that first year, so even though the distance was changed from year to year—it varied from a usual fifteen miles to an occasional thirty-two—and some years saw no finishers at all because of the cold water, the tremendous public interest enticed Wrigley to continue his sponsorship. And the swimmers knew a good thing when they saw it. There were professional races in other countries from 1927 to 1937, but the C.N.E. swim was the only big one, and these swimmers trained all year to peak in Toronto. They came from Australia, South Africa, Egypt, South America, Europe and the United States.

World War II postponed most athletic competition throughout the world, and marathon swimming was no exception. But when the professional swims were revived in the mid-forties, the C.N.E. was still the greatest attraction by far. This era was dominated by Clifford Lumsdon of Toronto. My trainer, Big Cliff. Cliff was the blond, blue-eyed, powerfully built prototype of the all-Canadian boy. His devotion to training was relentless and it paid off. His coach entered him in his first professional race, the C.N.E., at the age of sixteen, in 1947. He finished a very respectable sixth and moved ahead to fifth the next year. But 1949 marked the beginning of a seven-year stretch during which Big Cliff was just about unbeatable. He won at Atlantic City (a race around the island) and at the cold-water races in Quebec, and he even soloed across one of the toughest bodies of water in the world, the Strait of Juan de Fuca. He fought the sub-50-degree temperatures between Washington State and Vancouver Island and touched the shore in 11 hours, 35 minutes. But Cliff's real claim to fame was as indisputable champion of the C.N.E. He was on top from 1949 to 1955 and went out with many athletic records, along with the honor of being the biggest money winner in the history of the sport (a fact that still remains true today).

The clincher for Cliff was the last big one, 1955. Because Marilyn Bell had been the first person to swim across Lake

Ontario the year before (20 hours, 57 minutes, from south to north), that year's race was planned as a crossing of the lake, finishing at the C.N.E. in Toronto. The scheduled race day brought abominable weather, so the officials hurriedly set up a triangular course of equivalent distance, thirty-two miles, at the usual racing spot within the C.N.E. gates. The water was 49 degrees, and it was certain that no one would finish. The swimmers complained, but the date was not changed; sponsors come first. The water temperature was frigid hell; after twelve hours three swimmers were in the water; most of the others retired cursing the nearest official. Cliff had a healthy lead, and the sponsors gave him word through his wife Joan, who was his trainer, that if he stuck it out until the other two quit he would collect the first-place prize money without actually completing the swim. A couple of hours later he was alone in the water, but before he could stretch a frozen hand toward the gunwales of his boat, his wife relayed a new message to him. The double whammy. Cliff would receive no prize money unless he finished the thirty-two miles. He had just swum fourteen hours in 49-degree water; he had a serious chill, he could barely function, but he focused on one thought. He wasn't going to let those bastards screw him. He put his head down and stroked. The news went out all over Toronto, and sports-minded people started calling the radio station covering the swim. Cliff was promised the moon if he made it; one man promised him a lodge in the north woods, another pledged a new car, and another said he would cough up a dollar for every stroke Cliff took during the last five miles. Those last five miles witnessed a delirious, debilitated man, filled with desire. His legs were dragging toward the bottom; since he could only take three or four strokes before losing concentration, his handlers would scream and slap the water with oars to rouse him. The enthusiasm of the crowd grew to a bellowing roar; these people had loved the gentle winner, Big Cliff, during the past seven years, and the pitch of their emotion was letting itself be heard loud and clear. Cliff completed the entire circuit with a time of 19 hours, 42 minutes, collected a grand total of $84,000 and commanded the respect of a lifetime in his hometown. In Toronto today, more than twenty years after his 1955 glory, Cliff is still recognized wherever he goes. Strangers shake his hand, ask how Big Cliff is doing these days, or point to him across the street while describing to a newcomer the details of his incredible feat.

While the C.N.E. swims were the rage for distance swimmers this side of the Atlantic, a few English sponsors enticed some decent competition to race across the English Channel during almost every year of the fifties. During the fifties and sixties there were other races in Egypt, Italy, Argentina, Mexico, Syria and Canada, and even a few in the United States. However, when I competed, beginning in 1970, the general schedule was: one race in Australia mid-January; three races (two in rivers, one in the sea) in Argentina during the month of February; two races in the Caribbean area in March and April; the European races from the end of May to the beginning of July, plus a race down the west coast of Mexico during the last week of May; the cold-water races in Canada (mostly Quebec) for most of July and all of August; the Lake Michigan race the first week of September; and two races—one in the Suez Canal and another in the sea off Beirut—in late September. October 1 you went home to your family, studies, jobs and rest before the season started again.

As in tennis and golf (but with many fewer dollars involved), a commercial sponsor puts up money to operate a long-distance swim, and in return the sponsor is involved in whatever media time the swim attracts. In some countries, such as Egypt, where long-distance swimming is the national sport, the media time is significant; over 100,000 spectators line the shore of the Nile in Cairo as the best swimmers in the world wind a thirty-five-mile figure eight around two islands in the river. The swimmer competes for a percentage of the sponsor's contribution which has been designated as prize money. The pro circuit changes from year to year, depending on sponsorship of different swims and also on the political troubles in some countries.

BUCK AND I DECIDED my first professional race would be Hamilton, Ontario—a ten-miler in Lake Ontario in the middle of July 1970. It was a good choice for two reasons —it was short and it was nearby. (Since I was not yet proven on the pro circuit, I didn't receive air fare to the faraway places.) Buck and I arrived on the beach about an hour and a half before starting time, and I felt like a kid again in front of a big Disney screen. I was thoroughly enthralled with the colorful diversity of these swimmers. Amateur swimming suddenly seemed boringly proper and unimaginative; you raced in your own set lane against other women of nearly the same size and background to beat a clock by a few hundredths of a second. On this beach at Hamilton strolled ebony-skinned Egyptians with startlingly white teeth, followed by their trainers, who wore electric-blue, cardinal-red, and virgin-white caftans. The English, Dutch, German and Swiss swimmers wore immaculate sweats with the names of their countries emblazoned on the backs. The Italians and

Argentineans paraded around with their shirts off, flexing for the women in the crowd, flicking their long dark hair from their eyes. As it was the Canadians' and Americans' turn to wag their native tongues, they sought out the press, making sure that they capitalized on the location of the swim.

I was happily taken with the newness of all these characters, but I was shocked by their size. I had known beforehand that I would be competing with men, and mostly men, but I had never given any thought to the difference in brute strength involved. Even the ones who weren't especially tall were thick, muscular bears. Almost all of them, with the exception of a few skinny Argentineans, weighed upwards of two hundred pounds. And the women weren't exactly petite either. The women's world champion at the time was a Dutch woman by the name of Judith de Nijs. She was six feet tall and weighed 175 pounds; she had completely dominated the women's part of the sport during the mid and late sixties, and I could fully understand why. As I was securing my caps and goggles in place, she sauntered over to me and poked her enormous index finger into my chest. She said, "I hear you're very good svimmer. Vell, you're not going to beat me!" Somewhat intimidating.

The five-minute signal was given, all the great bears were greased (which rendered them even greater bears) and the ten-second countdown began. Everyone was supposed to wait for the "zero," of course, but I learned that day that a pattern of take-off was quietly assumed in all races. The Egyptians barreled down the beach at "ten"; the Argentinians and Syrians were on their heels at about "eight"; the Europeans gave it to a fair "three"; and the Canadians and Americans wouldn't budge an inch until the "zero" and the gun sounded forth simultaneously. For a swimmer who had always raced in a very civilized manner, I thought I responded to this alarming chaos exceedingly well, as if I might have a natural flair after all. Every time I was shoved headlong from the back, I gave an abrupt elbow in the ribs to the side. And for every Egyptian who ducked me five feet under to push himself ahead into free swimming space, I issued a return kick where it would be remembered most. The distance was ten miles, the water temperature was 62 degrees, and out of sixty professional swimmers, I finished tenth. Not a bad showing for the first time out. But better than that was the fact that I beat Judith that day (she never swam again) and I broke the women's world record with a time of 4 hours, 22 minutes.

In 1971 I was able to travel more than the first year, and in 1972, 1973 and 1974 I went to almost every race during the whole season (January to October 1). I was the best among the women and was officially world champion in 1974. The world championship is achieved, separately for men and women, by accumulating points, which are awarded according to the length and the difficulty of a swim, throughout the season. I had the time of my life, especially during the first two or three years, even though it was impossible to make a living. But at twenty-one, I really wasn't concerned with making a living. I got around the world five times, still managed to get through college and graduate school, broke several world records, made many solid friendships in addition to my rich relationships with both Cliff and Buck, swam with porpoises in the Virgin Islands, sea lions in Argentina and sharks in Australia. I would usually receive plane fare and expenses and my winnings would just about cover everything else, so breaking even was the best to be hoped for. I remember when the promoters handed me a

$500 check after my first race in Hamilton. I had been so proud and elated after the finish and my first world record that I had completely forgotten the purse. My only reaction was *And they pay me for feeling so good?*

But I'm afraid the wholesome naïveté faded fast. First of all, I quickly encountered really difficult marathons that didn't leave much room for humor. When I was paid $500 for crossing Lac St. Jean on a bitch of a windy day, my thoughts were more along the line of *A measly five hundred bucks for that hell?* Bobby Hull of hockey fame was the Canadian celebrity at Lac St. Jean that year; as he watched each spent body touch the finish marker and grimace with pain and fatigue while being hauled out of the water, he said, "You couldn't pay me a million dollars to go through that." After the first couple of years I began to take to heart the fact that I was busting my ass to train with top-flight discipline and to make it through these debilitating marathons only to break even. The emotional satisfaction was there and it was strong indeed, but a professional in today's athletic world develops another sense of pride by the money he earns. And if I was just breaking even as the world's champion, I wondered what was happening to the rest of the circuit swimmers. Some of them, especially those from Egypt and Argentina, were subsidized by their military or their government, and it is true that a year's worth of prize money will go much further in Cairo than in New York City, but we all had to face the reality that the promoters and organizers of the swims were getting rich while they dished out peanuts to the athletes. The same old story. We were put up in dilapidated school dorms where the walls didn't reach the ceiling or in open military barracks where sixty cots were lined up one next to the other. The prize money dropped to such low figures that it was nothing short of a humiliation to crawl out of the race, devastated by fatigue, and receive a check that would barely buy you dinner and an intravenous at the local hospital. I won a whopping $35 once in a ten-mile race, and as I was handed my check, there was an uncomfortable lump in my throat and a promise in my heart to remedy the situation or get out. I was not the only one.

Complaints grew into mass meetings, and the meetings grew into a new federation. Everyone admitted that ours was not a glamorous media sport and that we didn't expect to be making hundreds of thousands, but we had checked the books of the organizers and we knew that the swimmers should have been taking a much bigger share of the total purse. Our only power was that of a boycott. Dennis Matuch of the United States, Raul Villagomez of Mexico and Marawan Ghazzawi of Egypt were elected representatives for the swimmers. They worked very hard during the rest period of 1973 (October to January) to secure promises of increased prize money from the various swims by threatening 100 percent boycotts; but the problems were many. First, communication was difficult. Letters between Egypt, Argentina, Australia and the United States were not expeditiously delivered, and even when the letters were finally in hand, the differences in opinion caused problems. The Egyptians wanted to sanction the Capri–Napoli race because the Italians had upped the prize money a few thousand lire; the Americans disagreed because no plane fare was offered and a few thousand lire meant nothing next to a round-trip fare between the States and Rome. The Argentineans wanted to sanction their three swims in February because, even though the prize money stayed the same, the sponsors were going to send air fares to all qualifiers; but they refused to support the Canadian swims, the sponsors of which had raised their prize money somewhat without offering any air fare. And the Canadians were naturally of the opposite opinion. Ad infinitum.

For me, the final straw was Argentina in 1975. Buenos Aires was a delight to me, a South American Paris. The weather in February was sunny, and temperatures were in the eighties. The three races were good distances with good competition (37 kilometers in the sea finishing at Mar del Plata, tennis star Guillermo Vilas' hometown; twenty miles in the Río de la Plata, finishing in Buenos Aires; and twenty-two miles in the Río Paraná from Coronda to Santa Fe). I loved the people of Argentina, the food, the night life. And I especially loved the third swim in the Paraná River, as I had broken Greta Andersen's world record there the year before with a time of 8 hours, 23 minutes. (In my opinion, Greta Andersen is the greatest woman marathon swimmer in history.) And in 1975, after the leaders of the federation had made decent progress with most of the organizers on the circuit, I received my invitation with a one-way plane ticket, a promise of the return trip after the third swim, and an improved list of prize monies, starting with $3,000 for first and descending figures through tenth place. It certainly wasn't what we were shooting for, but change does not come about overnight; there was an improvement and I approved. I sent my acceptance telegram. It was a difficult time for me to take off for a month because I was in graduate school at New York University and the language exams were coming up in the spring; I had to pass fluency tests in French, German and Russian. I put in some extra studying and took several volumes with me.

I flew down to the coast for the first swim, slept off the jet lag and had a few good days of training in the ocean. After you've been swimming in indoor pools all winter, it is important to get to these ocean swims a bit early to reacclimate yourself to the surging of the sea. Also, it's wise to develop some semblance of a tan before the long swim; many a swimmer from the cold North has arrived late at one of the tropical swims and has had to be dragged from the water with second- or third-degree burns. The day before the swim, I was strong and well bronzed. The usual swim meeting was held at 5:00 P.M. so that everyone could be in bed at an early hour. All the swimmers and trainers meet with a couple of the organizers to go over the same rules with the same number of inefficient translations. Each swimmer is assigned a number and a boat with handlers. The swimmer must wear only regulation suit, cap, goggles and grease. The swimmer must swim to the side of his boat, not behind it. (Greta Andersen was once passed in a race in the Nile by an Egyptian with a wide grin on his face; he had a tight grip on a rope tied to the back of his boat, and was eating a banana.) The swimmer may not at any time touch the boat, the shore or another person. The swimmer will give a urine sample directly after the swim to test for amphetamines. A race official will be assigned to each boat to discourage foul play. If the swim must be stopped by the organizers due to hazardous weather and no swimmer finishes the race, prize money will be awarded according to position in the water at a rate of 50 percent. As this last rule was read off and translated eleven times, one of the astute Americans noticed a misprint on the sheet handed out at the meeting. He knew it was a harmless mistake, but chose to point out the humor in the error. The prize money was listed in pesos instead of dollars, as it had been on the invitations we received at home. Three thousand pesos was worth about twelve cents at the time, or an equally meaningless amount. Everyone had a hearty laugh until the unspoken truth settled over the room. The chief organizer pointed out that the mistake was in fact on the original invitation, and that the figures stood correct in pesos. The American jumped at the organizer's throat; he was somehow subdued and a heated four-hour argument ensued. The tentative result was that the swimmers would compete the next day if the prize money was on the up-and-up in dollars for the next two swims and if a fourth swim with equivalent money was added to the agenda. The organizers agreed, but the swimmers knew they weren't to be trusted. Most of us stayed up all night discussing what we should do for this swim and for the future. A boycott was tempting because this swim was a grand tourist attraction and no swim would mean thousands of dollars down the drain for the money men. But we were afraid to boycott because we thought they would then never offer the other races and would also renege on their promise of plane fares home. We envisioned ourselves on banana plantations for the rest of the year and showed up on the beach the next morning. Everyone was already exhausted, there was not an ounce of enthusiasm or adrenaline flowing anywhere, and the worst race in marathon swimming history began. Nearly everyone got out early, and the few who finished missed the satisfaction of having beaten the tough competition. Our immediate concern was the other swims.

We were in Buenos Aires a couple of days later, and it was evident that we had been royally screwed. All prize money would be in pesos, not even enough to measure up to the paltry prize money of the past. We had no choice but to boycott. Every swimmer agreed to stay out of the race, regardless of the consequences. But the morning of the swim, as we arrived at the start to put the organizers to shame in front of the public and to present ourselves to the press, a handful of Argentinian swimmers were greasing up. And a handful were just enough to make the swim successful. We whistled and jeered at them, but they took the plunge anyway and swam to minor glory in their country by winning and placing high in an international race in which they never otherwise would have stood a chance. Two overwhelming emotions filled me that morning as I watched those five swimmers stroke off next to their boats. First was a tremendous respect for Claudio Plitt. At the time Claudio was the finest swimmer in Argentina and one of the best in the world. He took a great chance by boycotting with us because he was in the Argentine army; it was a time when boycotts of Argentinian events were considered serious antinationalistic gestures. And he swallowed a great gulp of pride for the next week as the press hyped up the lesser Argentinians as the new champions. The second emotion that gripped me was a bitterness in knowing that my relationship with the pro circuit was near an end. The organizers had no respect for the swimmers, and worse than that, some of the swimmers had no respect for one another.

The promoters refused to give me my return ticket, so I spent an extra five weeks trying to persuade the American consulate to fly me home with a deal that I would pay them back within six months. I finally got back to New York, having both missed a considerable portion of the school semester and taken a dangerous loss of finances. I went to a few other swims in 1975, the ones I enjoyed, and when the summer season came to an end I was completely fed up. I decided to take my talent and my experience to some solo swims and to try to make a commercial success of myself.

3. Solo:
Manhattan Island

~~~~~~

As a young professional on the money circuit, I harbored a particular disdain for the long-distance soloist. Most of the other pros shared my prejudice; we were highly trained, tough, fast, solid (even the 200-pounders weren't of the blubber variety) competitors. Our idea of a marathon was eighty men and a handful of women making a supreme effort to outguts one another to the other side; we weren't interested in bobbing along, seemingly without pressure. The soloists were the ones who were too slow to make the pro circuit; they were often extremely obese. I always pictured them floating along slowly like great Arctic seals, insulated from the cold by their many layers of fat, until a giant wave washed them onto the beach at the other side. All of the circuit swimmers were quick to correct an outsider who might associate us with these tubbies. Except for an occasional English Channel crossing, which was necessary to save one's reputation with the public (who has never caught on to the fact that the English Channel is by no stretch of the imagination the most grueling swim in the world), solo swims were considered unworthy. We circuit swimmers were all unjustly biased.

I happened to be staying with a swimmer friend of the tubby species a few years ago in Victoria, British Columbia. When we would climb the stairs to his fourth-floor apartment I was afraid he would have cardiac arrest; red in the face, he would stop on every landing, sweating profusely and hyperventilating. As he introduced me around town to friends and media people as his fellow marathon swimmer, I would cringe with embarrassment. Toward the end of my stay we went for a quick dip in the Strait of Juan de Fuca. Water temperature: 50 degrees. When we surfaced after hitting the water, he seemed delighted and perfectly comfortable; I was numb from head to toe and couldn't get a deep breath. We swam out for about fifteen minutes and I zoomed way ahead of him because I was too cold to take fewer than eighty strokes a minute. I then turned around and met him again, and we were back at the shore within half an hour from the time we had dived in. Half an hour in 50-degree water and I was barely alive; my skin was scarlet red, I thought my eyes had frozen in their sockets, and I shook involuntarily for two and a half hours. My friend the Arctic seal had no trouble at all. His skin was only slightly pink, and he wasn't shivering at all; he didn't quite understand why I, with such a sturdy reputation behind me, was such a baby about a little cold water. I was confident he could have swum at least seven or eight hours, slowly, that day before the temperature would have penetrated his swollen epidermis.

The quick dip in the Juan de Fuca Strait was just after my first year on the pro circuit, and as far as I was concerned, the experience was the proof that confirmed my prejudice. All the soloist had going for him was sixty extra pounds of lard on his frame which anyone could gain if he so desired; I thought the swims they did could be done by absolutely anyone at all. The man who runs the 100-meter dash thinks that he is a truly gifted athlete and that the long-distance runner is insignificant as a competitor, since anyone who can finish is a winner; the long-distance runner thinks that success at the short sprint springs from a fortunate combination of genes and that his own kind should be regarded as the greater athletes because they display dedication, perseverance and a fiery show of guts along with god-given talent. Ironically, as a marathoner, I felt like the 100-meter dasher who thought very little of the slow, fat, plodding soloist. The athletes I respected were Cliff Lumsdon, Judith de Nijs, the Dutch speedster Herman Willemse, the great Greta Andersen and the legendary Abo-Heif. These were the top contenders just before my time. Greta Andersen, who swam in two Olympic games for Denmark, was a fierce competitor on the pro circuit. She was strong as a bull and intimidating as hell, and she beat every man she ever swam against at least once, a record that makes her the best female marathoner in history, past or present.

And Abo-Heif, Crocodile of the Nile, has left an unbelievable series of anecdotes in his wake. He was a character, an entertainer and a machine in the water. He spoke six languages beside his native Arabic fluently, he played the piano and sang at the after-swim festivities, and he would stick with the lead swimmer at any pace, for any number of hours, in any conditions, until the last five strokes, when he would beat the water in a flurry of windmill strokes and splash into the finish, yelling, "I win! I win! I am the first!" It was difficult to dispute, in any case. Abo was grand master at a trick known to distance swimmers as "catching a ride," swimming's version of running and cycling's drafting. If you swim very close to another swimmer, almost on top of him but a quarter of a body length behind, you will be able to ride his bow wave. He does all the work, encountering resistance as each hand entry meets "dead" (still) water, and you expend half as much energy because your hand entries meet already moving water. This may sound unsportsmanlike, but it is actually a smart tactical move. Many called Abo "the leech"; it was impossible to shake him off.

In a twenty-four-hour team race held in Quebec where two swimmers make up a team and supposedly split the swimming time equally, Abo's partner quit after less than one hour of swimming because of the cold water. Abo swam the remaining twenty-three hours by himself, nonstop, even though the other teams were stronger due to alternating rest periods. When his partner was given his half of the money their team earned, he handed it to Abo, but Abo wouldn't take it. He graciously said that they had made a contract as a team and that they would share the monies won as a team.

Abo was very near retirement when I started out in marathon swimming (his last year was 1971, at which point he was forty-six years old), but I clearly remember one incident. The night before a twenty-five-mile race across a Canadian lake, Abo broke his hand in a car accident. He wasn't at the official meeting and he didn't get to the motel until after midnight because the doctors at the town hospital had been setting the bones and fitting him for a cast. We had to get up at 2:30 to eat in time for a sunrise take-off. Abo showed up in the motel kitchen where we all scurried around in great confusion, trying to fix our different meals and prepare our food for the swim. Everyone questioned him about the cast, but he kept quiet and gorged his usual preswim fare of three whole roasted chickens, six scrambled eggs and ten or so slices of toast with honey. As the five-minute countdown was sounded at the starting pier, Abo began to wrap his cast in tight plastic coverings and to secure them with a dozen rubber bands at the wrist. Unbelievable. The hand was a definite hindrance, as Abo couldn't stay with the leader, but he did manage to latch on to a fellow Egyptian, Marawan Shedid, and beat him in by two minutes for a fourth-place finish. Abo-Heif's time: 10 hours, 9 minutes, 54.08 seconds. Shedid's time: 10 hours, 11 minutes, 41.06 seconds. The Crocodile of the Nile cherishes the longest-standing and most impressive record of any competitive marathon swimmer.

Abo, Greta, Cliff and the circuit gang from the fifties and sixties were my heroes; and the swimmers who inspired me my first couple of years in the sport were the best of my own contemporaries. There were nine of them, eight men and one woman, who were always strong, always tough. Each was best in a particular situation, a certain distance or water temperature, but a few of them persisted and succeeded at every hour of every race, regardless of the conditions. There were Horacio Iglesias and Claudio Plitt from Argentina, Raul Villagomez from Mexico, Jon Erikson and Dennis Matuch from the United States, Corrie Ebelaar and Johan Schans and Jan van Scheyndel from Holland, and a group of talented Egyptians led by Marawan Ghazzawi.

These were the durable bodies and the determined minds I had to contend with at every competition. None of them ever gave anything away; the races were never easy. In my book, the races were a demanding testing ground, while the

solos were in a league with flagpole-sitting. I had read about
Britt Sullivan, who was going to swim across the Atlantic
Ocean in 1964, swimming a few hours interchanged with
resting a few hours on a boat. She started at Coney Island.
Destination: the Portuguese coast. Twenty hours later,
somewhere off Fire Island in the dead of night, she went
under and was never found. And in 1931 another New
Yorker, Myrtle Huddleston, held the dubious distinction of
floating and occasionally swimming for a continuous 87
hours, 27 minutes, in a pool. Myrtle insisted afterwards that
she should go down as one of the all-time greats in the
marathon-swimming archives. A notch above Britt and
Myrtle was Argentina's Pedro Candiotti. His lifelong dream
was to swim the 300 miles between Santa Fe and Buenos
Aires in the Río Paraná. The water temperature of the
Paraná is 85 degrees minimum, and the average speed of the
river, which has been known to flow as fast as seventeen
knots, is eight knots. A swimmer can travel quite a distance
performing no work whatsoever by simply floating mid-river.
Depending on one's buoyancy, one can even fall fast asleep
on one's back in such a swift current while making considerable progress. Candiotti never reached Buenos Aires, but in
1935 he "swam" the 281 miles between Santa Fe and Zá-
rate in about eighty-four hours. The problem arises in deciding which to applaud, Candiotti or the Río Paraná. These
"drifts" are not recognized in the hard-core marathon swimming world; neither are swims made with wet suits, flippers,
flotation devices or other artificial aids. I had concluded that
a solo was generally synonymous with cheating.

Youth becomes more and more flexible, however, and I
came to discern the respectable solos from the flagpole-
sitting variety. Two factors helped me regard the legitimate

solo as a worthy enterprise. First there was Cliff, who as my trainer expressed to me in no uncertain terms the difficulty of his solo across the Strait of Juan de Fuca. And after all, Cliff's most grueling swim, his nineteen hours in the 1955 C.N.E. race, turned out to be a solo. Everyone had abandoned the race hours before he finished, and he says that the hell he fought through just to finish that one alone was ten times the hell he fought through in many races when a competitor's hand was slapping his toes right to the very end. The other factor which taught me reverence for the solo was my own experience. At first I thought the difficulty of the marathon was precisely that of any one-on-one sport; someone else (or more than one) a few meters ahead, a few meters behind or right on top of your shoulder meant moments of self-doubt. It was tremendous pressure to think, at a moment of weakness, that another swimmer was right there, just as fast, just as strong and maybe not feeling quite so bad. When you started the race, you knew that no one was as good, but when fatigue began to chisel at the body, paranoia simultaneously weakened the mind—a paranoia that gradually lowered your self-esteem. The only thing that saved you was flashbacks of yourself at stronger times when strength and confidence abounded; these gave you the perspective to know that your competitors were in trouble just as deep.

I still recognize this mental burden the marathon race creates, but I discovered that the most difficult and dangerous foe wasn't a fellow swimmer. No swimmer has more arms or legs or will power than I do. But the sea fights with weapons beyond my power to restrain. It requires a phenomenal demonstration of concentration to stick out hours of severe nausea, to continue stroking with efficiency for so many hours after physical pain has hit with full force, to resist the unbearable cold that saps your energy and distracts you from your objective. The mental and physical battle against another person is negligible compared with the battle against the elements. When a swimmer comes up to pass me after ten hours of racing, I may lapse momentarily into self-doubt; but essentially my response is one of self-esteem in knowing that if I was capable of staying ahead for ten hours, I am equally capable of staying ahead for fifteen or twenty or whatever is necessary. But when the waves rise to five-footers and hold for ten hours, I have no idea how long they will hold or if they will perhaps increase. I realize at the end of all circuit races that the pride I enjoy is in victory over the elements; the reason the marathon racers are so close for the most part is that they share that same victory over the elements even more than they relish the minor victories over each other. And I am certain that my triumph over Lake Ontario would have held the same significance for me if I had touched the other shore during a pro race, regardless of my finishing position. It took me a while to come around to this sort of thinking about solos, but I am now a full-fledged convert.

A couple of years before I came to appreciate the *real* soloists, I teamed up with Jon Erikson from Chicago in a twenty-four-hour, two-person relay race in Quebec. Jon was one of the steadiest, most reliable and most successful swimmers on the pro circuit. When he was fourteen, Jon was the youngest man ever to cross the English Channel (1969, 11 hours, 23 minutes, France to England), and in 1975 he became the fourth person in history to make a double crossing of the Channel. (The true weight of that story lies in the fact that he set a world record of 30 hours, 00 minutes,

previously held by his father Ted in 30 hours, 03 minutes.)
Ted was responsible for Jon and Cliff took care of me in
what we called "the twenty-four-hour Olympics." You swam
a third of a mile around a small lake in about eight minutes,
came into a floating dock, touched your partner's hand,
climbed out for eight minutes while he busted his ass
around, and then did your time again. For twenty-four
hours. Jon and I were holding a reasonably good third-place
position after twelve hours. But we had our eyes on second
as we were both steadier pacers, while one of the partners
on the second team was a sprinter/folder type. Some time
during one of my turns around the circle of buoys, I rammed
a floating wooden platform head first. I made it to the
exchange dock to set Jon off but I blacked out during his
tour. Cliff and Ted sent me off to the hospital and advised
Jon to slow down and keep swimming in the hopes that I
would be all right and able to get back in the water within
an hour or so. The doctors feared I had induced a concus-
sion, so they would not release me. Cliff tried to keep Jon's
spirits and strength up as he swam partnerless around Lac
St. Louis, and Ted came to see how I was doing in the
hospital. He saw that they weren't going to let me out and
he knew that I was feeling tremendous guilt, so he stayed
to comfort me. Ted is the type who very much lives in the
present—I rarely heard him re-create the great swims he had
done—but he picked the perfect time to tell me about one
of them, the Farallons.

The Farallon Islands lie thirty miles off the northern
California coast. In 1966, Ted attempted to swim from the
closest island to the Golden Gate Bridge in San Francisco.
Many had tried and failed before him. Sharks were a minor
problem, handled with a high-powered rifle, but the water-

temperature readings in the low fifties were the real stickler, especially for that distance. Ted pulled a chair up next to my bed and told me every excruciating detail of his Farallon attempt. (The moral of the story, for my benefit, was that even great champions encounter difficulties which can't possibly be outwaited or overcome.) He started out from the island one day in August. The water temperature was 52 degrees. Sharks appeared at almost every hour; the shots sent them away. And at almost every hour Ted weakened and faltered and almost lost consciousness. His friends and crew finally yelled and pleaded with him to abandon the swim. Only four miles from the bridge, after sixteen hours of painful determination, he passed out and had to be rescued. True to his reputation, he stuck around and tried again two weeks later, an attempt which he also had to abandon after ten hours because of persistent nausea. Ted capped his recounting of the Farallon swims by telling me that he made it the next year, 1967. He swam right under the Golden Gate Bridge in 14 hours, 38 minutes. (Ted also co-holds the record for the longest open-water swim in history. Along with Abo-Heif, naturally, Ted swam sixty miles in 1963, nonstop, across Lake Michigan from Chicago to Benton Harbor. That world record of open-water distance still stands firm today.)

Ted Erikson was not my only inspiration for solo marathoning. Kevin Murphy is another story altogether. Kevin, a young British reporter for the *London Daily Mail*, trains faithfully all year long and takes his few weeks' vacation in summer to tackle the most difficult swims on the other side of the Atlantic. And he has done them all. In 1970 he became the third person ever to double cross the English Channel (Antonio Abertondo was the first, Ted Erikson the second, Jon Erikson the fourth, and Cindy Nicholas of Canada became the fifth person, the first woman, and the record holder with an incredible 19 hours, 55 minutes). But Kevin did not leave it at a double crossing. He has tried twice to capture the three-way, a goal most swimmers take as an indication of deep psychological difficulties. One time he made a two and two-thirds, and if he ever gets a better break with the weather, the triple will be his. In 1971 he swam around the Isle of Wight, fifty-six miles, in 27 hours. And in 1970 he became one of the two people (Tom Blower was the other in 1947) to have crossed the difficult and freezing Irish Sea. The Irish Sea is often considered the most awesome swim in the world, an opinion backed by the number of failures the body of water draws. The difficulty lies in the murderous water temperature, which ranges during the summer months from a low of 47 degrees to a less-than-comforting high of 54 degrees. More world-class swimmers have been beaten by the Irish Sea than by any other expanse of water.

Kevin Murphy, both Ted and Jon Erikson, Cliff. I was hungry for a few solo titles myself. Nineteen seventy-four was Lake Ontario. And in 1975 it was Manhattan Island.

SEPTEMBER 24, 1975. I was lying semi-conscious on a cot in Brooklyn Hospital's emergency room. A doctor had quickly checked my vital functions and ordered two nurses to wrap me head to toe in warm towels. They struggled to inch my lanolin-soaked bathing suit down to my ankles, and the going was tedious because my skin was so tender from the cold. I was still trembling uncontrollably, muttering an incoherent stream of monosyllables. They packed my feet and legs first, moving upward, and the warmth of the 110-degree towels began to seep through my skin until the shaking subsided. I came around.

Less than an hour before I had been hauled from the chilly waters below the Battery in an unsuccessful attempt to break the record for swimming around Manhattan Island. It was simply a bad day. A hurricane that had been pounding almost every coast of the southeastern United States for the past five days had sent its nasty side effects up our way. There were severe flash floods throughout the New York area, the three rivers around Manhattan were flowing at a much greater rate than usual, and most important for a swimmer, the tides were considerably off their predicted daily schedules because of the high water level. The weather was unfortunate, for I was sure to break the record under normal conditions. I was in fantastic shape and the research I had done on this swim was thorough and accurate.

First and foremost, I had studied the hazard of Hell Gate, so called for good reason. All twenty-eight miles of river around Manhattan Island are fast-flowing (faster than any swimmer) and in some spots are subject to countercurrents and whirlpools, but nowhere is the situation as treacherous as at Hell Gate. The East, Flushing and Harlem Rivers converge between 88th and 90th Streets on the east side of the island, quite near the mayor's home, Gracie Mansion. The result of the three forceful rivers meeting, together with a very irregular bottom at that point, is a mass of wide-sweeping whirlpools that would be fatal for a swimmer during most hours of the day. Small craft have been sucked under the surface at Hell Gate, and a swimmer who was attempting to swim around the island in the early sixties was pulled under and thrown up again 400 meters to the north, thankfully still alive. The two opportune times of day for a swimmer to slip through this turbulent area would be at the two low waters, which occur twelve hours apart according to the tide tables for any given day. My plan was to start at Hell Gate at low water so that I would be assured of not having to fight the mighty whirlpools at their peak strength. Most of the successful swims around Manhattan had kicked off at the Battery at the southern tip of the island, but the record holder, Byron Summers, had jumped off at Hell Gate in 1927. It made good sense to me.

The next problem after Hell Gate was timing. Since I couldn't fight the tidal flow at any point, I had to approach each new segment of the swim as the tide was changing. Not only would I then be assured of good speed with the tidal assistance, I would have time to complete each of the three segments—the Harlem, the Hudson, and the East rivers— before the tide switched back against me.

I spent two days calling old swimmers who had made the swim during the past five decades. They were enormously entertaining with their exaggerated anecdotes, but they offered no useful information whatsoever. After that, I spent many hours with the New York Coast Guard, who were much more helpful. They even took me around the island on one of their boats at a slow enough pace to simulate my swim; I hopped in now and then to test the strength of the currents. We sat on the lawn of Governors Island, charts spread before us, and went over every possible combination of departure point, departure time and swimming direction. They had agreed with me: Hell Gate at low water would be the start. I would swim north in the Harlem River and then cut west to Spuyten Duyvil (the mouth of the Harlem as it flows into the Hudson); the ideal speed would be to cover the five miles in an hour and forty-five minutes. At that time, according to the tide tables, the Hudson would begin to flow down toward the Atlantic, so that the combination of my swimming speed with the three-knot current speed of the Hudson would allow me to travel the length of Manhattan in about three and a half hours. Once at the Battery, regardless of the tide situation, I could cover the mile or so to the base of the East River, marked by the Brooklyn Bridge. Following this plan, I would make the Brooklyn Bridge in some six hours, which would bring me to the East River just when it slows to slack water and then flows up at a strong speed toward the north again. I would make the Battery by five and a half hours, then pass under the Brooklyn Bridge at slack water and make my own headway for about half an hour; then when the fast current started to help me, I would race for 89th Street. I thought I could complete the circuit in eight hours, an hour faster than Byron Summers' record of 8 hours, 56 minutes.

Having checked the course plans over once more with the Fire Department tug captains, all I needed to do was gather a crew. My trainer, Cliff Lumsdon, agreed to come down from Toronto. Two friends from Michigan who had been on many swims with me before offered to help Cliff. A New York friend assisted me in securing provisions and equipment. My manager sent word out to all the press. As for an escort boat, I went to a few of the marinas around the city telling people I was going to swim around the island and that I was looking for a fun-loving boatman who would accompany me and take directions from my trainer. No money involved. It has been my experience everywhere else in the world that boating people, rich or otherwise, are high-spirited adventure seekers who would do anything asked of them to assist a courageous swimmer in challenging the elements. But in New York most of the boat owners refused to hear about the prospect without large sums of up-front money in pocket; the others simply laughed and motioned me away. They all knew I was a raging lunatic. When I approached Lou Wood from the *Today* show on his fancy yacht in the 79th Street Boat Basin, he waved his highball glass toward a beat-up lobster boat down the dock. The old boat was owned by a wonderful, soft-spoken old salt named Ed Linniger.

I boomed with my usual ebulliency, "Hi! My name is Diana Nyad. I'm going to break the record for swimming around Manhattan Island next week. Want to escort me with your boat?"

His expression never changed. "Doing it alone?"

"I'm the only swimmer. I have a crew of five: three trainers, a friend, and a reporter from *Sports Illustrated.*"

"Which day you thinking about?"

"Tuesday."

"Wednesday I gotta take my dog in for shots. Tuesday's okay."

So Ed Linniger and I went over the charts and tide books a couple of times and arranged to meet at the fire station on 89th Street on the East Side one hour before low water, September 24. Low water was at 1:05 P.M.

I was up at 7:00 A.M., fidgeting with the gear, checking it over for the twentieth time. Jars of grease, thermoses to be filled with hot water, cans of chocolate Sustagen, cans of sliced peaches, water thermometer, cups, spoons, glucose, extra caps and goggles, towels and blankets, bullhorn, flashlight, rubber gloves. Cliff, my three friends and I went over the course and the schedule again. I ate an enormous carbohydrate-loaded meal and we squeezed into a cab to arrive at 89th Street by noon.

The press was certainly interested. Every square inch of the sea wall was crowded: newspaper reporters scurried around with their spiral notebooks flapping, pens behind their ears; radio interviewers shoved their mikes in my face; and television crews tried to set up amidst the chaos. I spoke with them all. For some reason I was light and secure instead of brooding and worried as before most swims. When they asked me why, I answered, "Fame and fortune." When they asked why on such a miserable day, I said that nasty weather didn't faze me a bit. (The weather scared me to death, but this had to be the day; none of the crew could stick around, the weather forecast for the next four days was more of the same, if not worse, and the water temperature was dropping literally day by day.) At 12:45 I jumped onto the stern of the lobster boat, removed my sweat suit, socks and sneakers, and stood patiently as my friends covered me with six pounds of grease. In this swim I decided to use Iodex, a blackish heat-generating ointment that is actually rubbed into the muscles before the thick coating is applied. Except for my face and the palms of my hands (I try to avoid getting grease on my goggles), I was a beautiful ebony head to toe.

All watches on the boat were synchronized; they gave me the signal at 1:04 P.M., one minute before take-off, and began counting down by the second. I spit in my goggles and adjusted them to perfection. Dick Schaap said, "Good luck." Zero Mostel winked at me and said, "You can do it," and the gathering of interested onlookers were all shouting words of encouragement. Six, five, four, three, two, one . . . I blew Cliff a kiss, leaped from the stern of the boat into the water and paused before pushing off from the sea wall. "See you at nine."

I made it through Hell Gate and swam the Harlem River

segment with little difficulty. Passing through Spuyten Duy-vil (at 1 hour, 40 minutes) was tricky because of the currents, but after two unsuccessful approaches, I was in the middle of the powerful Hudson and making good time toward the Battery. I stroked into the Battery waters at 5 hours, 30 minutes, precisely on schedule. But something was wrong. There was pandemonium on the boat. I didn't need to be told that the East River tide had not yet changed or slack-ened as expected. I was caught in a very strong current. I tried treading water in close to the sea wall, but the rough chop was too dangerous. Out about fifty yards I had to fight like hell just to stay in the same place. After half an hour I was given the signal from the boat to try making it toward the Brooklyn Bridge, but the East River was still flowing toward the Atlantic so fast that I couldn't gain even a foot. I was being swept back toward Staten Island. At current speeds of three and a half to six knots on an average day, the East River at all times flows considerably faster than a swim-mer swims; and on this torrential occasion the flooding was producing an eight-knot current that rendered me helpless.

With great effort I made it back to the Manhattan sea wall. I spent another hour and a half treading and narrowly escaping the monstrous ferries that shuttled to and from Governors Island. The ferries couldn't easily change their course, not to mention the fact that they had difficulty seeing me and my small boat because it was then pitch black. It became more and more evident that the tide was going to be drastically off schedule. And although I hadn't found the water temperature unbearable while swimming up the Harlem and down the Hudson, I was extremely cold from the two hours of standing still with no opportunity to stroke and generate heat. The police boat pulled alongside my boat to speak briefly with Cliff. They concluded that the

East River was coming down at such a force to indicate that it would not reverse itself for at least another two hours. Even if I could have fought against being swept out to the Atlantic during that time, I would have been far from Byron Summers' record. (We found out later that night that the tide didn't change until nearly 11:30 P.M., five hours late.) I was not responding well; Cliff dived in and got me over to the police, who taxied me to Brooklyn Hospital.

The hot towels worked wonders, and forty-five minutes after being carried in on a stretcher, I was again feeling strong and ambitious. After all, this had not been the most demanding effort of my swimming career. Far from it. Bad weather had been the only reason for my failure, and there is no shame in that. The emergency room was brimming with laughter and anecdotes—and chaos. Cliff and my friends got dry clothes for themselves and had a warm drink. The doctors and nurses, also curious about my ventures, tried to restore order. And every media crew in New York crowded around my bed for an interview. Why had I picked such an awful day? Would I try it again? Why did I want to do it at all?

It was an awful day, and it was true that I had picked it. But there was very little choice in the matter. I had been swimming in Europe and Canada on the pro circuit during the summer, which meant I missed the warmer water months that are ideal for the Manhattan swim. I returned to New York on September 19 (the latest date anyone had ever done this swim, and it had been an inordinately warm year at that) and needed at least a few days to gather a crew and equipment and to study the tides and currents. Another factor was that Cliff had only a choice between the 24th or the 25th, which were identical in terms of weather. He had to be back at work in Toronto by September 26.

The only recourse would have been to wait a week or so until the flooding had slackened, but that would have put me into October. From all the past history I could dig up, the rapidly dropping water temperatures of late September and October turned a relatively easy swim (for a professional) into a near impossibility. All the successful swims around Manhattan had been done during July, August or the first week of September. The first man ever to accomplish the feat was Robert W. Dowling, who on September 5, 1915, got around after one disappointing effort a month earlier. Dowling's time was 13 hours, 45 minutes, and for 1915 it was an extraordinary swim indeed. (Dowling later became a Manhattan real estate magnate, and his daughter, Ruth Dowling, a psychologist, sent me a beautiful congratulatory letter after my swim in 1975, sixty years after her father's triumph.) One year later to the day the first woman completed the circuit. Ida Elionsky's time was a very respectable 11 hours, 35 minutes. There were others who made the swim during the warm months, but I will simply mention the male and female record holders. Diane Struble plunged into the Battery waters on August 15, 1959, and reached her original starting point in 11 hours, 21 minutes. And as mentioned earlier, the incredible kid from California, Byron Summers, set the all-time record in late July of 1927 with a final time of 8 hours, 56 minutes. This record held for an astounding forty-eight years until I set out to capture it.

There are several accounts of swimmers who tried to make the Manhattan swim in late September and October with much energy spent and very little success to show for it. Probably the most compelling story is that of Jazon Zirganos, a Greek army major who came to New York in 1958 to attempt circling the island, which by that time had earned a reputation as one of the tough swims necessary in a good long-distance swimmer's repertoire (along with the Channel, the Catalina Island swim and the crossing of either Lake Michigan or Lake Ontario). Zirganos had made it across the English Channel four times, had swum to and from every island in Greece, and had completed a few other decent swims in Europe.

He dived in at the Battery and plodded up the East River on October 5. The water temperature was 56 degrees. (On October 1, 1977, I took a short swim in the Hudson for a group of environmentalists. The water temperature was 68 degrees. When I had to take to the Hudson again for a magazine story on October 8, 1977, the water temperature had already gone down to 59 degrees. In early October the water temperature begins to drop by as much as two degrees a day; unlike air temperature, even a 2- or 3-degree drop can make a devastating difference to a swimmer.) Zirganos didn't set a very impressive pace because of the cold, and by the time he had emerged from Spuyten Duyvil and struggled a few miles down the Hudson past the George Washington Bridge, the wind was in his face. The temperature in the Hudson was 55 degrees. After more than twenty-three hours of continuous swimming, the frozen and unconscious Zirganos was dragged onto his launch and escorted to a nearby hospital, where he spent two days recovering.

Despite Zirganos' list of successful swims, it seemed that he did make a habit of overestimating his ability. Especially the last time. One year after his Manhattan Island nightmare the adventuresome Greek set out to cross the twenty-three-mile North Channel of the Irish Sea. Only two out of several hundred competent swimmers have ever made it across the unwilling and icy Irish Sea. Zirganos started out on September 27, 1959, and continued in a heroic effort which lasted some sixteen and a half hours. The end came suddenly. He stopped stroking with his face still in the water, and by the time the handlers could slip a towel under his belly to pull him up on deck, his skin was a cloudy gray-blue. The physician on board was alarmed and borrowed a pocket knife to open Zirganos' chest. He performed open heart massage for a number of minutes without success. Although there are very few such cases in the annals of marathon swimming, occasionally the cold has combined with the extreme demand of the exercise to overpower the heart.

No thoughts of Zirganos seemed to have been running through my head at Brooklyn Hospital, however. Once warm, I sat up all smiles, spouting witticisms at the press. Quoting Robert Browning's "a man's reach should exceed his grasp" and Captain Matthew Webb's "nothing great is easy" in the same breath. Exaggerating the attempt I had just made and understating the possibility of trying again soon. The water temperature had been 64 degrees that day, September 24, and everyone knew that it was cooling off at a dangerously quick rate. Yet there was one factor in my favor. All the work toward preparation for the swim had been done. The tide and current situation was known to be workable for any given normal day. The boatmen had just done an efficient run-through and were willing to stand by for the next go-ahead. There were no new provisions to secure; as soon as I was ready again the whole operation would also be ready.

Cliff, my three friends, the *Sports Illustrated* writer and

I shared a taxi back to my apartment in Manhattan. No one was depressed or disappointed, as sometimes happens after having to abandon a swim. The reporter said it would make a good story anyway. Cliff said it was a hell of an effort; it was just a shame about the hurricane; we would get it next year. My two girl friends from Michigan said it was the last straw, that I was bent on suicide, that they wanted no part of any future swim. All marathon swims were masochistic insanity and they had seen enough. I went to bed announcing that I was going to do it again in just a few days when I had regained my strength.

Unfortunately, what should have been a very short recuperation period from a relatively short swim became complicated by the fact that I came down with some sort of virus from the filthy water. Before the swim I had contacted the New York Board of Health and the New York Police Department, whose divers must be protected against the rivers' diseases. Both organizations recommended gamma globulin, typhoid and diphtheria shots. I had taken all three, and although I was especially cautious to avoid swallowing any water, one can't help taking in a minimal amount. Also, goggles sometimes leak slightly, allowing droplets to trickle into the tear ducts. In any case, I really had something. I vomited for hours that night of the 24th. A friend took me to get antibiotics the next day. I spent seven full days in bed, running a fever and losing weight. By October 1, I was up and about but feeling very weak and shaky. From what the New York environmentalists told me, I suppose I was lucky to get away with a ten-day virus.

By October 4, I was absolutely my old confident, cocky self again. I called Cliff to see if by any chance he could come down again. No chance, and I understood. Work is work. He wished me luck. I called my two Michigan buddies, who separately gave me the same line. "Now? In October? Why do you set yourself up for failure? Why are you punishing yourself?" They both gave me a flat, irreversible no.

It was too short notice to dig around the country for swimming colleagues, so I called a friend from *Esquire* who had been an interested bystander on both the first Manhattan attempt and on my Lake Ontario swim. She refused. She said she couldn't swim a stroke if I needed saving, and that she was incompetent in making decisions about course and waiting for tides and escaping strong currents. I told her that my mind was set; I would do the swim by myself if no one would help me. She accepted.

The forecast for October 5 was partly cloudy, chance of rain. October 6 was to be colder, in the forties, but clear and sunny. October 6 it was. Take-off from Hell Gate at low water. The press were again at 89th Street in full force. My zeal for conquering this record seemed to have captured the imagination of the public. (My theory was that everyone had been bored to death with the only two stories in the news for the past three months—Patty Hearst and the New York bankruptcy; my swim around Manhattan seemed wonderfully fresh and inspiring at the time.) Thousands had seen me fail the first time; and on October 6, everyone in the New York area was wishing me well.

Ed had his lobster boat ready, my amateur crew loaded their gear and waited on board, and the *Sports Illustrated* writer, by now a welcome crew member himself, joined us again. I was greased, this time with thick lanolin as it was significantly colder, and given the countdown from sixty seconds. Waiting in the water with five seconds to go, I appreciated the support of the public and the media. They were cheering and clapping; no one likes to play to an empty stadium. I waved and pushed off with a sprint to clear Hell Gate quickly.

The icy chill of the East River penetrated through the grease to my skin. From the first stroke I knew exactly what the next eight hours were going to bring: the fastest pace possible, shaking and stiffening with the cold, and telling myself over and over again that the water was 80 degrees. A delicious 80 degrees.

Hell Gate is tough, even at low water. The strong current takes your hand and pulls it through in whatever direction it chooses. You can't swim smoothly forward in a straight line; a zigzag is the result, but at least at low water it's a forward zigzag. I was out of Hell Gate within six minutes. The Harlem was like glass. I stroked a steady sixty per minute, and fifteen minutes ahead of schedule, I approached Spuyten Duyvil at one hour, thirty minutes. The Hudson was rough but the full force of the tide was with me and I almost frolicked in the waves. I stopped every hour on the hour for a hot drink. Very businesslike, on the way to a record, I grabbed the styrofoam cup and downed its contents within ten seconds. No talk, but I heard the cheers from the boat and saw the news helicopters hovering above. I passed under the World Trade Center buildings at five hours, twenty-five minutes. Perfect.

They headed me in close to the sea wall, and for the next half-hour I edged my way around the Battery, waiting for the signal to break full speed ahead for the Brooklyn Bridge. No hurricane this time; I passed under the Brooklyn Bridge at 5 hours and 56 minutes, and as far as I was concerned, Byron Summers' record was as good as broken. It was dark by that time and I was cold, but victory is sweet and I stroked toward 89th Street in high spirits. Fans lined the river. Traffic was jammed along the East River Drive as drivers pulled over to look down at the tired swimmer as she neared success.

I touched the exact spot on the sea wall that I had touched moments before pushing off. My time was 7 hours, 57 minutes. Except for the cold, I was in pretty good shape. The Fire Department let me use their hot shower, a friend tried to scrub the grease off my tender skin, and the press waited for me. Manhattan Island was mine!

4. Training

~~~~~~

FROM THE TIME I was eleven until I graduated from high school at seventeen, I decorated my bedroom walls with only two things. Two oversized posters with slogans written in thick, black ink. One read, THERE IS NO GAIN WITHOUT PAIN. The other philosophized, A DIAMOND IS A LUMP OF COAL THAT STUCK WITH IT.

I was motivated to excel at an early age. I am not certain if there was genetic influence, if the "first-child theory" was proving itself, if my early environmental makeup was ambition-oriented, or what combination prevailed. I am very certain, however, that I would have been damn good, if not the best, at anything I took seriously. My adolescent mottoes would have been the same regardless of setting or circumstance. Here's an essay I wrote at the age of ten as a fifth-grade assignment.

WHAT I WILL DO FOR THE REST OF MY LIFE

My mother says that her father lived to be 79. Her mother is still living. And my father's parents are still living. It would probably be a good guess that I will live 80 years. Which means that I have 70 years to go.

I want to see all the countries in the world and learn all the languages. I want to have thousands of friends and I want all my friends to be different. I want to play six instruments. I want to be the best in the world at two things. I want to be a great athlete and I want to be a great surgeon.

I need to practice very hard every day. I need to sleep as little as possible. I need to read at least one major book every week. And I need to remember that my 70 years are going to go by too quickly.

On first rereading my own essay, I shuddered to think what an unimaginative, achievement-thirsty little girl I was. But on second reading, I recognized the virtue of my passion. Even before I was accidentally introduced to a particular discipline, I was attracted to long-term goals, to sacrifice, to the pursuit of dreams. For a ten-year-old, I had a very keen sense of time—its passing, its fickleness, its limits. I had the drive, and drive will take you a long way; but drive alone, without talent, will not take you to the very top.

The tricky part of success is having the good fortune to find a field in which you are genetically gifted. Everyone asks me why I chose swimming instead of tennis. I didn't choose; it was environmental circumstance. I grew up within a certain educational peer group in Fort Lauderdale, Florida. Had I grown up in Minnesota, I might have been a speed skater; in Moscow I could have been a chess player; in Prague, I could have been a violinist. And then it was again chance circumstance that led me to marathon swimming. But when I consider the degree of excellence I reached in marathon swimming, I know that chance played no part in that at all. Many others had the same introductions and opportunities and some had equal talent and others had equal drive, but only a scant handful had all three.

Talent is a disturbingly amorphous concept to me—as is the term "natural athlete." The implication is that certain individuals are born with extraordinary gifts of muscular coordination, neurological efficiency, vision, brute strength and other qualities that enable them to accomplish the difficult feats of hitting a major-league pitch, serving a tennis ball at 138 m.p.h., running or swimming to world records. Agreed, certain individuals are born with these gifts, just as Jascha Heifetz and Vladimir Horowitz were born with the rare gifts that allowed them to pursue the violin and the piano to such perfection. My quarrel with the term "natural athlete" arises when hard work is overlooked. There are many children who have shown signs of promise, even of genius, but who haven't dedicated themselves over a life-time as has Heifetz. For instance, everyone spoke of Mark Spitz after the Munich Olympics as the perfect swimming body, the body naturally equipped with perfect symmetry, perfect flexibility, perfect fast-twitch muscle fiber, perfect flotation, perfect stroke. Spitz was seen as the perfect swim-ming machine. Little attention was paid to the fact that he couldn't have arrived at those seven gold medals without his self-discipline. That he worked his ass off four and more hours a day for fifteen years, that he had a very unsuccessful Olympic games in Mexico City, that he worked twice as hard in preparation for Munich—all this was of less interest than his natural talent. It is true that many violinists have practiced as diligently as Heifetz throughout their lives without reaching the pinnacle of virtuoso performance because they lack ability. And there are literally hundreds of swimmers who work just as hard as Spitz did with comparatively minor results. If we are speaking of the very best in the world, in any area, the champion is made by a combination of superb talent and uncompromising long-term dedication. But I am convinced that the combination, among most champions, is not a fifty-fifty situation. Many of the champions in the world of sport were and are slightly deficient in some area of natural ability; but it is unheard of at the top to find an individual oozing with talent without a past history of ardent work. Most champions have put in thousands of extra hours in improving deficits or in strengthening their assets in order to overshadow their weaknesses. The endurance sports are the prime showcase for this theory—even minimal talent can couple with relentless drive to equal success.

As an endurance athlete, I consider myself reasonably endowed with natural talent. My average resting pulse is about 47 beats per minute, and I have registered a resting pulse of under 40 several times in my life. (An average pulse is 72 and the average pulse for a full-time athlete is about 60.) My pulse recovery rate is excellent: I can take my pulse to over 180 with about ten to fifteen minutes of hard work on a rowing or cycling ergometer or with a few 100 percent efforts of running or swimming; within three minutes my pulse returns to about 65 and within five minutes it is at 55. Even most well-trained athletes require twenty to twenty-five minutes to lower their pulse to within 10 beats of the resting rate after having taken it over 180. My lung capacity has been measured at 6.1 liters, which is more than twice the expected capacity for my size. (The average capacity for my size is under 4 liters.) A large lung capacity is helpful because you can breathe fewer times per minute to fill the lungs with oxygen.

But, above resting pulse, pulse recovery rate or lung capacity, the single most significant indicator of cardiovascular fitness is aerobic capacity. Aerobic capacity is also known as aerobic power, cardiovascular endurance or VO_2 max. This is the measurement of the highest oxygen uptake an individual can attain during strenuous physical work. It indicates how efficiently the oxygen transport system is getting the energy-producing oxygen to muscles at the cellular level. VO_2 max is measured in milliliters of oxygen per minute, adjusted to body weight (ml/kg/min). It is a somewhat time-consuming and complicated measurement to take, which is why we more often refer to pulse measurements as indicators of cardiovascular fitness. And pulse is an appropriate indicator; it's just that VO_2 max is the most accurate indicator of all. My VO_2 max, when swimming heavily, is 69.2 ml/kg/min. It means that I am feeding oxygen very efficiently to the muscles at the cellular level. A decent VO_2 max for a full-time athlete would be about 42 ml/kg/min. Endurance athletes are generally higher, and some cross-country skiers have been tested at about 80 ml/kg/min. In any case, 69.2 is quite high.

Also, I have quite an efficient system of caloric usage; during my heaviest swimming months I can consume up to 12,000 calories per day without any weight gain. The average daily caloric consumption is 2,000 to 2,500. Very active athletes, expecially males, take in about 7,000 a day.

Specifically for swimming, I have two genetic advantages that enable me to perform well over a long distance. First, as my earliest coach recognized, my muscular coordination is good, which gives me a feel for the water. This has allowed me to develop an efficient stroke (analogous in running to a natural, rhythmic stride, which allows the runner to waste little energy while moving forward most efficiently). I have a strong kick, so I ride high in the water and create a constant bow wave with the momentum of my head; I have a long and strong stroke, which means that I glide forward at a maximum distance for every full arm rotation; and I swim at a very steady pace with concentration on balance, so I can continue for many hours without straining one muscle group beyond its functioning capacity.

The second genetic trait that makes me a good swimmer is my body symmetry. For my size and weight, 5 feet 6 1/2 inches and 130 pounds, I have extraordinary strength in my upper body. At the weight room I always perform excellent sets of lats (the fanlike muscle that stretches from under the armpit to the middle of the back), triceps (the extensor muscle at the back of the upper arm), deltoids (the large shoulder muscle group), biceps (the contracting muscle at the front of the upper arm) and pectorals (the chest muscles). Then I am relatively poor in developing strength or mass in the lower body. I am sure that swimming all these years has contributed to this proportion (as it has developed my cardiovascular capacity), but when I see pictures of myself as a child, I see that it was always so. Well-developed shoulders, arms, back and abdominals with underdeveloped legs, gluts (ass) and hips. Most land sports (the high jump and the pole vault are the two exceptions that come immediately to mind) require a low center of gravity for balance. In swimming, the higher the center of gravity, the better. The surge forward through the water comes almost entirely from the power of the upper body. (Robert Cossette, a French Canadian who lost the use of his legs, has successfully swum across the English Channel). Any mass, whether in the form of muscle or fat, on the lower body acts as drag. The legs and hips should be as lean as possible and serve for body position and balance as the torso rotates on its axis.

I am grateful for having inherited an amount of natural ability. But my pride lies in my courage. Churchill said that "courage is the highest of all human virtues." I am proud to have developed both the courage to attempt difficult feats and the courage to persevere through difficult months and years en route to those feats. I have swum twenty hours in Lake Ontario, forty hours in the North Sea, and on sheer guts, I have beaten some of the top men in the world who were stronger and faster than I. My fastest running mile to date has been 5:12, which is not particularly impressive. However, on the same track I have run twelve consecutive miles in under 72 minutes, or better than 6 minutes per mile. And I have run twelve one-milers with a one-minute rest between each, with a result of the fastest being 5:41 and the slowest being 5:52. I vomited for the entire minute's rest after the eighth mile but had the will to finish the last four in good time. I have skipped rope at a good pace for a continuous hour many times. I can enter the squash court and practice drills, shots, racketwork and footwork for four and five hours at a time without breaking concentration. And, most important to me, I have found enough energy to chase my athletic dreams with no concessions, however slight, without excluding other dreams, nonathletic ones.

There is no doubt that the overwhelming drive behind my success is that I am absolutely unafraid of pain. I am willing to put myself through anything; temporary pain or discomfort means nothing to me as long as I can see that the experience will take me to a new level. I am interested in the unknown, and the only path to the unknown is through breaking barriers, an often-painful process. The expression used in swimming is "hurt, pain, agony and ecstasy." It is not pain for pain's sake. If someone is willing to confront the unknown and break pain barriers, a pattern will eventually reveal itself. The unknown will begin to define itself, and the number of barriers one must face before success will become more and more clear. The process is self-serving: each plateau is increasingly difficult, but each new plateau one reaches renders one better qualified to reach the next.

When I was first swimming seriously at eleven, I was never late for a workout, I never skipped a workout, and I never had any preconceptions about a workout, so I arrived prepared to handle anything. I am still the same way today. Since I started marathon swimming in 1970, I basically divided the year into two parts—the season and the off-season—and except for the yearly flu and a couple of colds, I am in excellent condition every day of the year. The season means the actual competitive weeks of the long swims and the direct training months leading to those swims. Because swimming combines very poorly with other sports and land exercises due to the vastly different muscular involvement, I usually do nothing but swim during the season. (I keep up with strength training during the season, but not as extensively as during the off-season). As I mature as an athlete I constantly reassess my training technique, my psychological approach to training, and the new barriers I pass in training.

I include three basic types of aerobic training in my weekly schedule during the season. In order of importance, they are intervals, fartlek training and LSD. Intervals are sets of any distance—let's say twenty 200-yard freestyles— with a short rest in between each repeat. (A repeat would be one 200-yard swim in the set of twenty.) Fartlek means alternating fast laps (at a 75 to 80 percent effort) with slow laps (at a 30 to 40 percent effort) without stopping. LSD is long slow distance swimming. For example, an average week would be five hours a day Monday through Friday in a pool. Two hours in the morning of middle-distance intervals. Let's say sets of 200, 400, 800 and 1,000 yards with a certain rest interval between each repeat. (Intervals are done at approximately 85 percent performance rate.) Then one hour of 100 percent 50- and 100-yard sprints in the middle of the day. A lot of rest between each repeat so that I am working at close to maximum capacity. And two hours of fartlek in the afternoon. For example, I might go a 200-yarder fast, a 100-yarder slow, a 200-yarder fast, and so on. Then on the weekend I will do two LSD swims in the ocean or the pool as the weather dictates. LSD swimming is done at about 65 to 70 percent effort; for instance, I might swim eight straight hours on Saturday and six straight hours on Sunday and return to intervals on Monday.

Any one of these three types of training, if done methodi-cally and regularly, will result in a good level of aerobic conditioning. I have found that for the very long swims, all three are necessary for the highest level of performance. First, a change in the type of workout is imperative. No matter how difficult an exercise is, if you do it every day, several times a day, for months and months, it will at some point become easy. If the workout is easy, you're not making any progress. The second reason for all three types of train-ing is that each type serves a different purpose. The inter-vals, which take the pulse rate higher than either fartlek or LSD, are for intensity. Intensity is probably the single most important factor toward making gains in fitness. The higher you take your pulse and the longer the period for which you take it up, the better you are training your heart to work efficiently under stress in delivering large quantities of blood (and thus oxygen) to the rest of the body. If your muscles are constantly rich in oxygen, they can perform better and longer for you. The intensity of an interval workout also makes the heart more efficient at rest because it has learned to coordinate its fibers better in wringing the blood out of its chambers and because it has grown in size and strength through the constant wringing of large volumes of blood. At rest, the heart will have to beat fewer times per minute to deliver the same volume of blood to the rest of the body.

Fartlek training isn't as important as interval training to me, but I find that it does help in two major areas. First, it is a way to raise the pulse during the fast laps (although not as high as during interval work because such intensity couldn't be maintained during the length of a fartlek workout) and then, one hopes, lower it during the slow laps. Fartlek accustoms you to spurts of intensity such as would happen during moments of a competitive race or even a solo —where you might have to swim quickly out of the path of an oncoming ship or a giant school of jellyfish—without draining you so that you are then capable of returning to a comfortable pace without stopping. Fartlek also teaches you a sense of your own pace. Without glancing at the pace clock you know just how fast (I can guess my times to the tenths of seconds), and how slow, you are swimming.

LSD is just as important to my kind of sport as the two other types of training, but I find that too much of it is not productive. You would perhaps think that if I swam six hours every day of the week, regardless of pace, I would be getting more benefit than from five hours five days a week with longer swims on the other two days. But if I swam six LSD hours every day, I would be sacrificing intensity altogether, and as I said, intensity is probably the single most important factor toward making gains in fitness. Long slow distance would not be enough on its own, but for endurance athletes it is necessary a few times a week. If I am preparing for a swim of about twenty hours and I never do anything but sprints in a pool, I am grossly neglecting two aspects of preparation. One is specific muscular endurance. Until the deltoids, the lats, the triceps, the neck and the hip flexors (the major groups of muscles that take considerable strain after a few continuous hours of swimming) are put through several straight hours, they will never build in endurance to withstand the pressure that comes after eight or so hours. (In running, the well-trained middle-distance runners are probably in good enough aerobic shape to complete the twenty-six-mile marathon; but if they haven't been putting in the continuous distance, the muscles and joints of the legs won't be able to stand the pounding on the pavement for so many miles.) LSD is important for another reason— psychological preparation. After you are in great condition, after you have groomed the correct mental attitude toward approaching pain barriers, the mental strain of the long swim is the most devastating of all. And this is an area in which practice helps just as it does in the physical training. The more long training swims you have under your belt, the more you have grappled with the hours, with yourself and with the ultimate solitude in which you are immersed, the better you will cope when the big day comes.

During both the season and the off-season, cardiovascular training is first on my list of priorities, but I also take strength training very seriously year-round. I've been lifting

some sort of weights since I was twelve years old. Not only
is weight training necessary for any serious swimmer, but it
is an essential part of fitness for anyone.

There are basically three methods of weight lifting, which
potentially offer the same results. One is free weights
(dumbbells and barbells), which you lift through the air
against gravity to weaken different muscle groups. (The first
step to strengthening a muscle group is to weaken it.) I used
free weights until I went to college and had access to a
Universal gym. The Universal gym equipment consists of
one large mass of weighted plates with bars attached. You
move from station to station around the bars, pushing and
lifting in different directions to weaken the different muscle
groups. The Universal has one great feature over free
weights; it is safer because all the plates and bars are secured
to one another, whereas free weights are a potential danger
without supervision. (Most discus throwers and other field
athletes, however, stick to free weights because they can
simulate the movement of their sport with the dumbbells.)
I used the Universal gym for six years until I discovered
Nautilus equipment.

I was working out on a Universal gym one Christmas in
Florida when a handsome, Greek-bodied young man shook
my hand ferociously for three minutes while explaining that
he knew exactly why I was taking such good care of my body.
He said I was making sure that my body was in a state of
perfection so that it would be ready to make the transition
when the glorious day of the afterlife came. What could I
possibly say to that? The next day he took me to a Nautilus
center to introduce me to finer delights for the body, and
I have been hooked ever since. Nautilus is a brand name for
a series of machines, each of which you strap yourself into

so that one muscle group at a time is isolated and can be worked alone until it's exhausted.

The Nautilus equipment has three virtues over free weights and the Universal. First, because of the rotary cam to which the plates are attached by a pulley (the cam is in the shape of a Nautilus seashell), the resistance changes throughout the movement. For instance, if I want to work the biceps with a barbell, I sit in a chair, grab the bar with arms fully extended in front of me, palms up, and bring the bar up until it rests under my chin. And I repeat that movement until the biceps are no longer capable of lifting the bar. But with a barbell, because I am physically able to lift more weight in the position of leverage at the chin end of the movement, the weight I choose to lift is never appropriate. One weight will be perfect at the beginning, weaker segment of the movement while too light at the chin end; and another weight that would be perfect at the chin end would be impossible to hold up in the extended position. As the cam of the Nautilus machine rotates, the weight lessens or increases according to your position of leverage. Every Nautilus movement also allows the muscle group to move through a wider arc, and thus provides about 25 percent more range of motion than any other type of resistance training. There is more stretch in the beginning of each movement, and there is a greater arc of motion throughout each exercise. One of the chief complaints about weight lifting is that it tightens the muscles and reduces flexibility. As one who is extremely inflexible, I can attest to the fact that since I started on a Nautilus program, I have never been more flexible in my life. The third Nautilus virtue is that most Nautilus training centers in the United States are set up as a one-on-one situation. No one trains alone. A trainer has your chart, is sincerely involved in your cardiovascular and strength improvement, and takes you from machine to machine, from an ergometer such as a stationary bicycle, which keeps the pulse high, back to a machine, demanding your very best effort at every station. Unfortunately, for all its assets, Nautilus equipment does not have mass availability in its favor. It is quite expensive, and because you need at least one machine for each separate muscle group, it requires more space than free weights or the Universal.

In the final analysis, however, the type of equipment is not of ultimate importance. The point is to find some way of imposing resistance on one muscle group. Let's say you begin with the quadriceps (the front of the thigh). You need to lift that weighted resistance as many times as necessary until that muscle group is too spent to lift again. Depending on the person, the amount of weight and a few other factors, that magic number may be three, twelve, twenty, or more. The number makes no difference: what does is proper form combined with the muscle group working to exhaustion that counts. After the quadriceps, you put the hamstrings (the back of the thigh) through the same routine, although a different weight may be required. You continue to exhaust muscle group after muscle group, emphasizing areas of weakness or vulnerability or flabbiness, until you have worked the entire body. Muscle growth is a complicated process; suffice it to say that this type of isolated exhaustion will stimulate growth and will cause increased strength.

I am a great advocate of strength training, at all levels of fitness, for both men and women, for all age groups. One minor reason to activate the big muscle groups is that they can help directly in cardiovascular training. When a muscle group is engorged with blood as it is when used in intense exercise, it contracts strongly and efficiently to send that blood back to the heart so that it will again receive a reoxygenated supply. If several big muscle groups are demanding blood rich in oxygen, they are all squeezing blood forcefully back to the heart. The heart muscle gets a terrific workout because it is forced to meet demands at the other end. So raising the pulse is not exactly the goal; if you were frightened horribly three times a day, which made your pulse zoom up to 200 and stay there for five minutes, you would not see the same results as if you skipped rope three times a day for five minutes when your muscles and your heart were busy squeezing blood back and forth. But the real reason behind strength training is that the muscles atrophy without stimulation. The muscles are like the engine of a car. Other parts of the body serve other functions, but only the muscles can set you in motion and perform work.

Some sort of strength training is obligatory in a fitness program, as far as I'm concerned; and I find that the old taboos against women and weights are now reversing themselves. First of all, because of hormonal flow (basically the flow of estrogen and the lack of testosterone), very few women are capable of developing any noticeable muscle mass. Weight training for women seems to be the perfect answer to firming and toning problems. I also happen to think that weight training provides a necessary psychological lift for women. It gives you a sense of your own power, a confidence in the competency of the female body, a pride in your stature and a healthy vanity about your development.

I don't look at the off-season as rest time. Quite the contrary. I put in many hours, usually seven to eight a day, during those months when I am not swimming in order to maintain the highest possible level of both cardiovascular and strength fitness. I have always thought that the only difference between the season and the off-season for me was that during one period, I was swimming, and during the other, I was not. I felt that my fitness level was basically the same throughout the year and that it was simply a question of transferring cardiovascular and strength assets as the exercise switched with the season. But I have discovered in the past few years that this is not the case. I am much more fit when I am swimming. For example, the day I am writing this is March 6, 1978. On July 1, 1977, I began the off-season training for the longest swim of my career (the longest open-water swim in history) from Cuba to Florida, which will take place in July 1978. Since the swim is 130 miles and will require over sixty hours of nonstop swimming, I projected a year of serious training to be necessary. I was in good shape before I began. From July 1, 1977, to February 27, 1978, I did little to no swimming because I would have been bored to tears. With the exception of several weekend squash tournaments, my daily athletic schedule (I was writing, carrying out some business transactions and engaged in other activities besides sports) for that period was as follows: a twelve-mile run at a six-minute pace or the equivalent distance in intervals in the early morning; two hours of squash alone during the midmorning; a one-hour squash match midafternoon; one hour skipping rope at 5:00 P.M. or the equivalent time in intervals; a one-hour squash match in the evening; a Nautilus weight workout twice a week; and a half-hour of push-ups, leg raises, chins, dips and lower back raises on the off-Nautilus days.

Monday, February 27, was the day I had designated to stop all land exercise (except Nautilus) and begin swimming. When that day came, I felt I was really prepared. The previous eight months had been time well spent: my resting pulse was just over 50, I was stronger than ever before in my life, and almost nothing could make me tired. After one week of swimming—only one week of four hours a day—my resting pulse has gone down to 43, the muscle groups of my upper body are pumped up to twice their size, and I am so exhausted that I slump into a deep sleep at the library, at the breakfast table, at the dinner table, all day.

I realize that every athlete offers his or her sport as the ultimate in everything. Frank Shorter or Bill Rodgers can cite statistics to prove that long-distance running is the greatest possible aerobic workout. Arnold Schwarzenegger will swear to the fact that there is no comparable overall workout like weight lifting. Suzy Chaffee will make the same claim for downhill skiing. Every nouveau cross-country skier will glibly remind you that his sport rates higher as an aerobic exercise than running, rowing or swimming. And swimmers are well stocked with their own arsenal of statistics. Swimming has long been at the top of the list for developing pulmonary and cardiovascular efficiency. And, of the aerobic exercises, swimming requires the least amount of time to secure the same results. Also, there is no other aerobic exercise you can do while utilizing as many muscles of the body at one time. Even if all things were equal between swimming and running, rowing, skipping, skiing, cycling and the other aerobic exercises, swimming still has lack of injury on its side. You can swim without gravitational force on the joints and muscles. Injuries are rarely induced by swimming; as a matter of fact, swimming is often recommended by physicians for orthopedic, arthritic and cardiac problems.

In my own experience, I haven't yet come upon a sport

or an exercise which, if pursued with even a modicum of frequency and intensity, is capable of devastating the body the way swimming does. To my knowledge no land workout is as difficult, as painful or as productive as a tough swimming practice. Swimming is demanding of so many systems at once, and it is exactly because of its high demands that the benefits are so varied and so rich.

There are two major drawbacks to swimming, however. One is that, however superior an exercise it is for the heart, the lungs, almost every muscle of the body, the mind and the joints, it has a disastrous effect on reflex action. Word has it that the managers of football teams in August gather the team members together (Joe Namath excluded) to give the first pep talk with the ensuing dos and don'ts. "I don't care what you eat, how much you sleep, who you sleep with, what you wear, what you do about the length of your hair. But you better show up at every practice on time, and *nobody swims!*" Even in training for sprint swimming, you are basically floating in the prone position for hours at a time. Balance on land becomes difficult. Swimming is a sport of rhythm and continuous applied pressure, not of quick contractual movements. Most good land athletes can switch sports and fare reasonably well, but swimmers rarely double as proficient land beasts.

The second drawback is that swimming for any length of time is without a doubt the most boring exercise imaginable. Take it from someone who knows. Everyone thinks that all the Olympic swimming champions hit their physical prime at about fifteen. Preposterous. It is simply that 99.9 percent of all world-class swimmers start extremely young. They don't particularly enjoy their years of practice because swimming lap after lap in discomfort, with no communication, with no change, is not enjoyable. Swimming, as an amateur sport, is goal-oriented, and all the time spent—sometimes upwards of a decade—preparing for that moment is basically hard work. Moreover, women have few opportunities to continue training at a world-class level after high school age —as opposed to men, for whom a great deal of scholarship money and good coaching is made available. (Marathon swimming differs in that the long swims themselves are learning processes, enlightening experiences and sometimes money-making propositions; but the training toward those swims is still unsociable and boring, and basically hard work.) The physical prime for sprinting probably comes when a person is twenty-six or twenty-seven. The physical prime of the marathon swimmer seems to be somewhere in the early or mid thirties, similar to other distance sports. How the distance swimmers cope with that extra decade of monotony is not readily explainable. Perhaps it's because they make their living by the swims. Perhaps it is the unique personality of the marathon athlete to cope with monotony longer and better than the sprinter. In any case, the fact that swimming laps becomes boring is not limited to the world-class competitors. Even the ordinary person just trying to keep himself or herself in shape finds swimming boring if done frequently enough. After all, there are no distractions. Even while running, the casual jogger can take an apprecia-tive glance at the scenery and can chat briefly with a friend or a stranger. My recommendation to those keeping in shape is to swim because swimming is invaluable, but to alternate swimming with running, skipping rope, cycling or any other exercise that demands raising the heart rate for the duration of the exercise.

No one needs to imitate my program to keep fit. My sport

is an extreme one, and I am an extremist. But everyone
should strive for basic fitness for its own sake, an idea fatally
ignored by most of the American spectating public. It is
forgotten that the body atrophies and deteriorates significantly faster when not maintained. If you don't set out to
maintain it yourself, there is little physical demand in our
society that will maintain it within the life style. It is forgotten that the mind functions more smoothly and with better
endurance when the body is maintained, and that one's
emotional life also runs more smoothly. And it seems to be
forgotten that everyday life can become a playground of
sensual awareness when the body is fit and well tuned.

A minority of people—mostly joggers—are changing all
that. Some of them turn to me for reinforcement, for expla-
nations, for training ideas. Whether in a letter, a phone call,
at the track or squash club, or in the many locker rooms I
manage to frequent, I meet at least one serious nonprofessional athlete a day who would like me to lend him or her
advice on setting up a particular fitness program. Sometimes
I feel like "The People's" coach. And I love it.

One of my immediate projects is to operate a fitness
center in Manhattan where nonprofessional athletes could
be trained by professional athletes and coaches. With a pool,
a track, weight equipment, ergometers and jump ropes, the
center will be a serious one and the atmosphere will be
intense. No juice bar, no vibrating belts, no socializing.
Women and men can come in and be tested for percent of
body fat, resting pulse, heart rate recovery, VO_2 max, muscular strength and flexibility in all the parts of the body.
Each individual would indicate how much time she would
be willing to spend, and whether that time was one hour
weekly or one hour daily, a program would be designed for

her by me and my staff, and she would be guaranteed that if she promised to show up regularly, we would promise her superior physical fitness in return.

Another of my immediate projects is a basic training book that I am just now beginning with a sportswriter friend, Candace Lyle Hogan. A major part of the book will be directed toward women in a high-powered attempt to demythologize many of the physical taboos which have been forced upon them for centuries. But the thrust of the book is not gender-related: detailed analysis of the heart and lungs in their relation to aerobic and anaerobic exercises; strength training and its relation to aerobic fitness; a look at thirty sports and exercises to see what muscles they develop, what level of aerobic fitness they effect, what injuries they might cause, and so forth; and specific workouts for people from ten years old to ninety (excluding medical cases) with allowances made for age, past history, motivation, schedule and activity.

Right now I do a ridiculous amount of strenuous physical exercise—a regular working day's worth. (I always say that my intellect will blossom in my thirties. And my mother always asks when I am going to abandon this adolescent behavior and lead an adult life.) In any case, physical prowess won't be the center around which the rest of my life revolves forever, for physical fitness isn't everything. I won't always be making my living as an athlete; I won't always be training eight hours a day. But I am very certain that I will be extremely fit every day of my life.

The body actually doesn't require much time to maintain the pulmonary, circulatory and muscular systems; and for every minute you devote to its maintenance, it will repay you a thousandfold. Remember, in developing your body, the two key words to fitness at any level are regularity and intensity. I have already expressed my opinion about intensity. One hundred percent efforts will yield the greatest results. The problem is that 100 percent efforts can't be given often for both physical and mental reasons, so the next best thing is work done at 80 to 90 percent effort. (I consider endurance to be an extension of fitness. It is possible to be quite fit and still lacking in endurance qualities. For superior endurance, you need the intensity and regularity for basic fitness; and then you need the continuous hours of 65 to 70 percent effort as well.)

Regularity speaks for itself. The body is a systematic machine, as is the mind. If you practice the clarinet once a week for three hours at a time, you will make one-tenth the progress than if you practiced thirty minutes a day six days a week for the same total of three hours a week. The brain is much better equipped to store and recall information to which it is frequently exposed than information to which it is exposed only occasionally. And if you run six miles every Sunday, you will make fewer gains in fitness than if you run one mile every day, at 80 to 90 percent effort, six days a week. The body has a memory, too. Fitness is a compilation of daily results. Of course, if you have been extremely active all your life, you will be in better shape than the forty-year-old who just started a fitness program one month ago after twenty years of inactivity. But strictly speaking, when one is tested scientifically for VO_2 max, lung capacity, heart rate recovery and the other measurements that indicate fitness, one's level is basically dependent on the nature of one's activity during the past four to six weeks—a feather in the cap of regularity. If the heart, the lungs and the major muscle groups are stimulated properly every day or several times a week, the effect is cumulative, as if each part remembers and easily recalls what it so recently learned.

I suppose the third most significant word in a fitness program is variety. In the same way that regularity is necessary to learning, intensity is lessened with regularity. If a one-mile run is intensely difficult at an 8:00 pace, it will become less and less difficult if you tackle it every day for a few weeks. After a few weeks you would have to quicken the pace to 7:30 to ensure intensity. Or you would have to raise the distance to two miles and attempt to complete your run at the same pace at which you ran one mile a few weeks before. One method of guaranteeing intensity, then, is to constantly make the goals more difficult. Another method is to mix up the types of exercises you include in your program. This is antiproductive to a professional athlete or someone who is competing seriously in one sport, but for people for whom physical fitness is the main objective of exercise, a change in activity works wonders. Swimming, running, rowing and cycling make use of different muscle groups, demand different levels of strength, and require different amounts of time to reach the same results. But to the general fitness person, they all serve the same purpose: they force the pulse up for a continuous activity, they force the heart to deliver large quantities of oxygen through the blood to the large muscle groups, and they raise the respiration rate so that more oxygen is continuously available. As long as intensity and regularity are not sacrificed, a combination of the aerobic exercises for variety would be ideal.

When considering fitness, some people think only of aerobic capacity and nothing else. In my book, as I have already explained, fitness involves muscular strength as well. My formula is to take the number of hours you devote a week to general fitness and divide it in the following manner: 70 percent to cardiovascular activity to consistently raise the pulse and expand the lungs; 25 percent to strength training to stimulate the major muscle groups through resistance; and 5 percent to flexibility or stretching exercises to prevent stiffness, soreness and injury. The proper combination of these three activities will also help you to maintain another important fitness factor—body weight.

Body weight is an overwhelming American preoccupation. It means nothing whatsoever to me. It is lean muscle mass that serves a purpose, just as the body fluids, the organs and the bones obviously serve their purpose. But body fat, after allowing a minimal amount for reserve and insulation, serves no purpose. If I weigh 130 pounds with 11.2 percent body fat, I will tax the heart and lungs less in providing fuel for movement and I will tax the muscles less in their efficiency of movement than if I weighed 120 pounds with 22.2 percent body fat. The measurement of the body fat ratio can be done in several ways, the most accurate and technical involving floating in a scientific displacement tank. Another simpler method is the calibration of a skin-fold measurement. In any case, it is not a readily accessible statistic for the average person, so the next best step is to study your lean muscle mass over the entire body in the mirror. Men on the average have about 10 percent less body fat, and because of testosterone production, have a greater tendency to develop muscle mass and definition. So when you are looking in the mirror for taut, firm muscle groups with accentuated definition, don't compare yourself to anyone else, man or woman. Even among both sex groups, genetic traits influence the ability to define. Mesomorphs, who tend to be thick and muscular, will show clearer "cuts" than ectomorphs, who

tend to be wiry and nonmuscular; but the average meso-
morph doesn't necessarily have a lower percent of body fat
than the average ectomorph. Just look at yourself for fat and
fluff and know that every extra percent of fat is not carrying
its own weight and is taxing the other systems to carry it.

If all the rules of fitness were strictly applied—intensity,
regularity, variety, 70 percent cardiovascular work, 25 percent weight work, and 5 percent flexibility—a reasonably
effective program could conceivably involve no more than
twenty minutes a day. Twenty minutes out of every twenty-
four hours for a richer life. My hope is that through my own
example, fitness centers and books, I can persuade more and
more people to give those twenty minutes. And for those
who already give their twenty and more, I hope I can still
be a help by encouraging, teaching and making myself available. As a marathon runner friend and physical-fitness director, Robert Glover, says, "We don't guarantee to add years
to your life, but we will add life to your years."

5. Mount Kilimanjaro

〜〜〜〜〜〜〜〜〜〜〜〜〜〜〜〜〜〜〜〜〜〜〜〜〜〜〜〜〜〜

AFTER MY RECORD-BREAKING swim around Manhattan Island in October 1975, I received over a thousand letters. Strangers who were inspired enough to take the time to put pen to paper. Half of the letters were from men, men who said they admired my courage, who said I reminded them of themselves years ago, who said they wished to God more of my generation were like me. The men seem to identify with the fulfillment of potential. Their letters say it; their faces show it as they gather at the shore to witness my exhausted but successful emergence.

The other half of that fan mail came from women. Courage was again the key word, but instead of identification, there was longing. "I wish I could do something great in my life." "What I wouldn't give to burst out of my cocoon and tackle any one of my dreams." The women seem to envy the adventure, the extreme. They seem to thrill to this one young woman's courage, as if she were carrying the burden of all womanhood's ill-spent time. As if she were exploring her potential a thousandfold for the women who can't yet see how they might explore their own.

One of the strongest sensual memories I consistently have after the long swims is of the women on the shore. Wide-eyed, open-mouthed stares. Egyptian women, Italian women, Argentinian women staring in wondrous disbelief as if their souls are awakened by the power of my act. The desire is ablaze in their eyes, but they have not yet set themselves free.

The long-perpetuated image of women as subordinate, dependent and weak is by no means past history—but an ardent battle to change that image is in full swing. Women are proving their competence and their intelligence, moving quickly and strongly into every area of adventure and creativity that was previously a male stronghold. Women should realize, are realizing, that their lives are their own. How is an individual to seek her potential if she is un-reservedly devoted to someone else's search for his own?

I am a feminist. I like to think that I am a model for women who are beginning to discover and to display their strength. When I was ten, my father smiled at my brother, who was watching TV, gave me a pat on the fanny, and told me to run along into the kitchen and make the salad. You should understand that my father is a big, muscular man who in the true Greek tradition believed in a few lashes to set his children straight. I made a salad for five and I made it as wet as possible, with many tomatoes and avocados, extra oil and vinegar. I marched toward my father's chair, other-wise known as "the throne," and overturned that wet salad in his great, Greek lap. This was not a little girl angry with her father nor a young person rebelling against an authority figure; this was a female recognizing at a tender age that she was going to demand her own space and her own time regardless of social precedent. Lashes ensued, but nothing so painful as acquiescence.

Women, thanks to the advocates of Title IX et al., now have the law on their side, and they are beginning to muster the confidence to pursue their own rights. Probably the weakest realm left is the physical one, and ironically enough in this age of technology, the fulfilling of her physical potential is one of the biggest steps woman must take toward commanding her 50 percent in all domains. It's not a question of equaling men in brute strength, which is unreasonable in any case due to hormonal and structural differences, but one of a strong and confident self-image, which develops from a sense of physical prowess and self-awareness. If women had more physical experience, the constant occasion for physical expression, they would be in better touch with themselves. And being in touch means the ability to tap and to control a wider variety of resources, to delight in a richer life. After all, we are animals at the core, however intelligent, and physical competence is the solid groundwork for competence and confidence in other areas.

Until very recently, the few women athletes fell into one of two stereotypes: either they were unsightly, muscle bound freaks who were supposedly unhappy as females and trying to prove themselves otherwise, or they were the unique Babe Didriksons and Wilma Rudolphs who were respected as gifted aberrations from the norm. But in the 1970's, women athletes revel in an era of reverence and superstardom as never before. The improvement of women's performances in all sports at the world-class level is astounding, and probably the number one factor behind these strides is the new opportunity for youth participation. There is encouragement at an early age, there is adequate and professional coaching, more and more inspirational role models are stepping into the limelight, and there is even money for women's sports. Scholarships are finally available. Before 1974 no colleges offered official athletic scholarships for women. For the 1977 school year more than four hundred colleges offered more than 10,000 athletic scholarships worth more than $7,000,000 to young women.

And even though most adult women today didn't have an encouraging introduction to sports, or to exercise, for that matter, it seems that they are diving into the physical world anyway. There are over 5,000,000 women jogging around the country. Can you imagine how many women sported track shorts and sneakers and went pacing around the tracks, down the streets and through the hills of the 1950's? Women are buying 20 percent more athletic equipment than only ten years ago. Women are beginning to pay attention to their bodies as physical specimens, sources of energy, and functional machines. Women are even pumping iron in gyms and health clubs all over the country as they realize that muscle tone is not a singularly male vanity.

The President's Council on Physical Fitness and Sports publishes an annual national health survey which in recent years has indicated that women are exploring their physical selves as never before. As a matter of fact, in several sports, women outnumber men as participants. As of 1975, the total number of cyclists in the U.S. was 14,854,000; 8,001,000 were women. And of the noncompetitive tennis players in 1975, women made up 8,139,000 of the 14,965,000 total participants.

Soon it may be common knowledge among women that physical development and experience and expression are the

logical forerunners to other means of success. Even as early
as 1891, Frances Willard, addressing the National Council
of Women of the United States, said:

Be it remembered that until woman comes into her kingdom
physically she will never really come at all. She has made of herself
an hour-glass, whose sands of life pass quickly by. She has walked
when she should have run, sat when she should have walked,
reclined when she should have sat. . . . She is a creature born to
the beauty and freedom of Diana, but she is swathed by her skirts,
splintered by her stays, bandaged by her tight waist, and pinioned
by her sleeves until . . . a trussed turkey or a spitted goose are her
most appropriate emblems.

Women read about female politicians, cancer researchers,
corporate executives. They admire these ambitious sisters,
and their hearts warm to the thousands who are taking
action in the move toward equality. But the physical domain
is the last male bastion, and the female athletes are still
untouchable visions to be stared at with wide eyes and open
mouths. Billie Jean King, in her win over Bobby Riggs and
in her unswerving demand that women tennis players be
paid equally with the men (and hence be respected equally,
as money and respect go hand in hand in the American
sports arena), helped woman's positive image improve by
leaps and bounds. Janet Guthrie, participating in 1977's
famous Indy 500, proved the value of sticking with years of
doing what she wanted against the impossible odds of the
greatest male chauvinists of them all, car racers.

When I swim up the North Sea or down the Nile, or
across Lake Ontario, I feel I am the Diana who represents
freedom to the women waiting on the shore. Men and

women both are touched and inspired by the courage of an individual who would not give up. But the women alone are moved by the unique physical strength of a young woman just like themselves.

And I in turn am moved by other unique, physically strong women. The most inspiring case was a woman I met on Mount Kilimanjaro.

THE PEAK OF MOUNT KILIMANJARO is 19,340 feet high, the highest in Africa. The climbing of Kilimanjaro is not a technical feat, where the subtle and difficult art of handling the rope, picks and all the new sophisticated equipment is necessary. It is not a trained climber's challenge, but it is certainly a rugged, exhausting confrontation for the individual lacking in climbing expertise, even if he has a certain amount of strength, a good deal of endurance and boundless determination. It is ordinarily a six-day venture, four and a half days to the top and one and a half days back to the base camp. Whether you go it solo, with someone or in a group, you must hire a guide.

In 1974 I spent three adventuresome months in Africa, partly in French West Africa and in the northwest region between Dakar and Casablanca; for the most part, though, I joined my mother in the rich and wild animal kingdom that is Kenya and Tanzania. I had just finished six months on the regular marathon swimming circuit and had been invited to Africa for a few more marathons, so I was in fabulous shape. I was up at dawn, swam for miles in the ice-blue Indian Ocean, followed elephants and leopards and marabou storks during the day (and vowed never to patronize a zoo again), ran for miles along the coast at night and put in two hundred sit-ups and two hundred push-ups before bed. The three months came to a close all too soon, but on

my next-to-the-last day in Nairobi, a young American couple
told me about the Mount Kilimanjaro climb. They gave me
literature about the time, equipment and expense involved,
and I knew immediately that I wasn't going to let this
experience pass me by.

The next day I flew down to Arusha in Tanzania, a short
bus ride from the Kilimanjaro base camp. As I had been
prepared for swimming, not mountain climbing, I had to
rent all the gear: boots, socks, sweaters, parka, gloves, visor,
caps, poles, lip and skin salves, toilet paper. I hired the guide,
who would carry my food supply and advise me what and
how much to eat as the altitude became a problem. I was
to meet him the next morning at 5:00. I took a run into the
town, some five miles away, ate dinner, walked back and
went to sleep romanticizing about what might happen in
this Hemingway domain. But I never for a second questioned my physical ability to complete the climb. It simply
didn't seem so difficult. The literature reported that children
had done it. And after all, wasn't I the Superwoman who ran
twelve tough miles every morning, who did a thousand sit-
ups at the wink of an eye, who defeated rivers, lakes and
oceans left and right? Mount Kilimanjaro was going to be
a piece of cake.

The guide was waiting for me in the morning; we shook
hands, and I was delighted to discover that he couldn't speak
a word of English. (My Swahili was something less than
fluent.) I relished the prospect of spending six quiet, intro-
spective days in this mountain paradise; from the first step
I sank into a blissful and undisturbed reverie. I followed a
few paces behind him; he would occasionally point to an
animal or a bird and we would stop for short drinks or light
meals, but generally he kept to himself and I kept to myself.

The first day was more of a walk than a climb. The

temperature was in the eighties, so I wore only a sports shirt, jeans and sneakers and carried the heavy gear. We reached the first hut before sundown. We ate and I wrote in a pamphlet. I was enjoying the solitude, the chance to day-dream and sort out my past and future, but I was becoming more and more disappointed in the climb. There wasn't even a glimpse of a challenge.

A few hours after setting off the next morning, it became cooler; I put on an extra layer of clothing and the paths gradually became more steep. The whole venture took on a more respectable light. About 4:00 P.M. a figure appeared some few hundred yards ahead of us; the image was of that of the ant carrying an entire slice of bread on its back. As we approached, I saw that it was a very old woman who was walking hunched over to the point that her back was almost parallel to the ground. She was carrying along the length of her back an enormous bundle of steel and bamboo rods and rolls of tree bark, all secured together with banana-bark ties. The bundle must have measured five and a half feet in length (at least six inches taller than she was) and was about three feet in diameter, so that it seemed as though its very weight would crush her frail bones. If I had had to guess her age, I would have ventured a conservative eighty. She had deep creases all over her face, her limbs were thin and seemingly delicate, and her voice was feeble and cracked. My guide saluted her and she lay her bundle on the road while they chatted for a few minutes. I couldn't understand a word. I pointed and gestured toward the bundle, asking her permission to lift it onto my back, curious as to how much weight this petite grandmother was hefting up the mountainside. She smiled a toothless smile, giving me the okay, and I slipped my fingers under the banana ties, preparing to hoist the whole load easily over my shoulder. I couldn't budge it. I shook my head, faced it again in disbelief, got a better grip and still couldn't budge it. I had lifted weights since I was twelve years old, and although as a swimmer I wasn't trained to lift huge amounts of weight, I was strong. Since I knew that I could take at least 150 pounds from the ground, even if I couldn't get it over my head, I estimated this steel-bamboo-bark bundle to be at the very minimum 150 pounds. I was amazed to think that this emaciated eighty-year-old could handle more than yours truly, Superwoman. Both the old woman and my guide indulged themselves in a hearty laugh over my inferiority. I shook her hand with true admiration, she slung her load onto her back and we started off again.

The third day became uncomfortable as the oxygen level thinned and the cold began to bite. The clothes I'd rented at the bottom were of the Mickey Mouse variety. I had to stop more and more often, as the hills were quite steep and the thin air was making me nauseated. And the fourth day was still tougher. I vomited everything, liquid as well as solid. I felt dizzy most of the time, my legs occasionally gave way beneath me, and I was bitterly cold. I tried to decide whether I had ever been that cold during a marathon swim; the verdict was yes, but it didn't seem to help. Three of my toes were frostbitten, both my feet and my hands were numb, and I was shivering uncontrollably. That fourth night was an unforgettable nightmare.

We arrived at the camp after dark. I was so fatigued and weak that I cried a bit at the sight of the hut and tried to concentrate on the prospect that by sunrise the next day I would be at the summit and on the way home. I tried unsuccessfully to get some bouillon down. It was 9:00 P.M., and we were to start the final ascent at midnight so as to reach the top before the day's cloud cover enveloped the peak. I met up with thirteen Danish, Swedish and Norwegian men who worked at the medical mission in Arusha and thought they should tackle Kilimanjaro before their time in Tanzania was up. We were all freezing and huddled together in the hut (which, by the way, was missing one wall so that the wind came howling through our holey sweaters and parkas). Except for the 10-degree-below-zero cold, the men all joked about the ease of the climb, saying it was nothing to write home about, and after having been put to shame by the old woman, I was feeling less and less like Superwoman all the time. The three hours of waiting in that open-faced hut were sheer discomfort, and I was thrilled when my guide came around. The Scandinavian group weren't going to set off for another half-hour, so we left without them. It would supposedly be six hours to the top, and exactly as in all marathon swims, the time passed excruciatingly slowly. Six hours seemed like twenty-six, and the end never seemed to come into view.

Most of those last six hours were over jagged, snow-covered rocks. Often I would slip or my boot wouldn't find a flat surface, so I was constantly on my hands and knees. Several times an hour I would fall on my knees to vomit, and the guide would kneel next to me, pat my shoulder and whisper *"Polepole"* (slowly). He believed I could make it if I just advanced a few feet at a time, waiting each time for the dizziness to fade and then trying a few more feet. Something I had also learned from marathon swimming was that the sunrise gives you renewed confidence and strength; when the sky began to lighten from black to midnight blue, I knew I would make it. The guide said *"Polepole"* over and over again, and at 6:15 I stood at the top and witnessed a sunrise that made me wish I could paint. Deep purples, magentas, soft blues, forest greens, screaming oranges and yellows and flamingo pinks stretched across the sky for more than 180 degrees. All the lower peaks of Kilimanjaro jutted up around me, and I truly felt like King of the Mountain. I reexperienced all the exhilaration of swimming the long, difficult distances. I had climbed this mountain with my own arms and legs, my own will power. I conquered it myself.

I signed my name in the book, hugged my guide and suddenly didn't feel as cold or nauseated. Victory works wonders! A few minutes later I heard some voices and stepped over to the edge of the glacier to see who was coming. It was one of the Danish doctors, talking to a friend just behind him. The friend was sick. I yelled to them in German that they were a mere 200 feet from the top, but they stopped for a long time and finally began descending. Twenty minutes later my guide and I began the descent also. We came to that infamous fourth hut in two hours' time, and the whole Scandinavian group was there. Not one of them had made it all the way. My guide and I continued down, feeling better, even drunk, as the oxygen became more abundant, sort of skiing through the volcanic ash with the walking sticks extended to help in balancing. By sundown we were at the first hut, where we were scheduled to spend the night before proceeding to base camp the next morning. But I signaled to the guide that even though it was dark, I wanted to get back that night, and he was just as willing. We almost ran the last four hours home. I had my feet taken care of, soaked in a hot bath for two hours and made arrangements to fly over to Dar es Salaam first thing in the morning. Back to the sea, back to my medium.

When paying the proprietor in the morning, I asked him if he happened to know of the old woman I had met on the second day. He said she worked for the Tanzanian government and for more than six months had been climbing Mount Kilimanjaro once a week, every week, leaving her load of building materials near the top for climbers and botanical and zoological expeditions. She was paid approximately five cents a day.

I flew off to play in the Indian Ocean and afterwards to running, swimming, reading and writing in the Canary Islands on the way back to the States, and I thought about that old woman every day. In my society, where everything is mass-produced, mechanized, catered to convenience, and where people have nearly completely forgotten the beauty of the power that their bodies wield, I stand out as a prime physical specimen. True, the jogging revolution is here and it is good. Americans are finally considering nutrition as it relates to the quality of everyday life. Eyes are opening; the first step is being taken, but it is not enough. I am still one of the few Americans today who appreciate the muscular, cardiovascular and pulmonary systems not only as works of art but as efficient and effective machines. And yet I am incontestably overpowered and outdone by an eighty-year-old woman who is a product of a thoroughly physical society.

6. Sensory Deprivation

~~~~~~

SOMETIMES WHEN I'M SWIMMING, especially after a number of hours, I feel exactly as though I am in the middle of a night dream, in a hallucination beyond my control. When soldiers in war, exposed to loud and terrifying bombing and forced to go several days without sleep, complained of similar hallucinations, doctors seriously analyzed this "sensory deprivation" for the first time. They found that the soldiers' memories became confused, their perceptions of what was real and what was imaginary were distorted, and if certain sensory functions were severely damaged, they might have been unable to perform the simple physical skills of walking or talking or shaking hands. I have experienced the same symptoms in the long swims.

To the psychiatrist, the neurologist and the neurophysiologist, sensory deprivation is more of an experimental term than a description of a real-life situation. The favored theory for years was that without stimulation the brain would fall asleep. After all, in the Western tradition one enriches the

mind by bombarding it with as many stimuli as possible
during a lifetime. Without stimuli, then, you deprive the
mind. One neurophysiologist by the name of John Lilly
brought in a countertheory with a big bang. I first read Lilly
through his experiments with the intelligence and language
of dolphins. From then on, I kept an eye out for his name,
and when the material on sensory deprivation came out in
full force I was tremendously relieved. For many years, both
during the hours of laps for sprint swimming and then
during the long hours of continual swimming for the marathons, I had been experiencing what I considered to be very
bizarre trips. I had gone through entire LSD trips without
the drug (I took several acid trips to compare the experiences) while swimming, but I couldn't find another swimmer who was interpreting his experience in the same way.
I had no reinforcement, no friend with whom to converse
and learn. When I read Lilly's material on sensory deprivation, I realized that what I had been going through on the
long swims was the most successful experiment of all. I just
hadn't known how to label it or how to begin to carry over
its effect into my everyday life.

In the experimental sense, sensory deprivation means cut-
ting off all the senses from outside stimulation and leaving
the brain to its own devices. Lilly's method of doing this was
to float for a number of hours in a large tank filled with an
extremely dense solution so that the body would float very
high. He would float on the surface with the room darkened
or with dark goggles over his eyes. This is obviously not the
same as sitting in a dark room for hours in a chair. He
discovered that if the water were kept at 93 degrees, he
wouldn't be able to differentiate hot from cold and his
tactile sense wouldn't function. His hearing would disap-

pear, as his ears would be just under the surface and no
sound waves were being produced in the tank. Lilly and
hundreds of others (myself included) floated in his tanks for
varying lengths of time, and each individual experienced the
same phenomenon. The brain didn't go to sleep; when de-
prived (the term should be changed in this case to "left in
peace") of sensory stimulation, the brain is vitally active.
Everyone who came out of the tanks said that he'd had very
vivid daydreams and seemingly wild fantasies; and everyone
said that he felt rested.

Is this beginning to sound like self-hypnosis? Self-hypnosis becomes successful when you can entirely block out all
outside stimuli and bring your mind to a pinpoint focus on
one thought or one sensory image, such as a blinking light.
When that pinpoint focus is complete, the mind is free to
travel and to remember and to imagine much better than
when it is inhibited by the duties of ordinary sensory attention. And when the hypnotic trance is over, you feel as
though your mind has been immensely creative at the same
time that you feel wonderfully rested. Just as floating in a
sensory deprivation tank produces many of the same effects
as self-hypnosis. Both of these techniques are reminiscent of
some forms of Eastern meditation in which you recite a
mantra or chant certain syllables until you shed layer after
layer of external involvement with the environment. When
you have reached your core, and outside stimuli can't penetrate, your mind and your spirit leave your body on a free
adventure. They later return to your body, and the overall
sensation is security and tranquillity.

Many overactive Westerners would like nothing better
than to let their minds take a creative (and safe) trip while
automatically rejuicing with energy, but they find the sen-

sory deprivation tank somewhat inconvenient, self-hypnosis a bit frightening, and Eastern meditation hard to swallow in any form. This is where sports come in. Most sports require a concentrated focus and a shutting out of outside stimuli. As the founder of California's Esalen says, "Sport is a Western yoga." Aside from physical fitness, sociability, and the particular pleasures than come with specific sports, many people participate in sports on a casual level for the mental freedom and relaxation they provide. (Recent studies show that clinical depression is treated with a high degree of success by exercise programs.)

And on the higher levels, sports become a true meditation ground. The favorite word in sports these days is "automatic." Her tennis swing is automatic, his left uppercut is automatic, his golf swing is automatic, her skiing style is automatic. Of course, going on automatic pilot is considerably easier at the higher level of sports, after you have practiced the routine thousands of times so that the body can perform without conscious instruction. The beginner must constantly remind himself to "get the racket back, hit the ball in front of the body, put the body weight into the stroke." But the world-class player will undoubtedly play better if he can completely eliminate all outside stimuli, including his own conscious voice. When he sees the ball approaching over the net, his eyes focus on that spinning seam; he doesn't hear the crowd, he doesn't notice the heat, he just switches to automatic pilot and performs with the grace and speed of a cheetah. This is concentration, self-hypnosis—in effect, sensory deprivation. In tennis, the masters of concentration are Evert and Borg. It is always said that they never change expression; they apparently are not emotionally involved, which is another way of saying that their focus is so intense and so pinpointed that it precludes other levels of awareness. (It is odd that Chris Evert is referred to as "the ice dolly" while Bjorn Borg is called "the king of concentration" for displaying similar degrees of focus.)

Other athletes at the upper levels experience the same phenomenon. They practice for years until their specific movements become automatic, and at a moment of peak performance, they tune out all outside stimuli and do the job better than ever. A few quarterbacks have spoken of stepping back from the center as if floating in slow motion through a choreographed ballet; it seems as though time has stopped, all sounds have vanished, and the pattern of their movement toward releasing the ball is clear as crystal. Skiers recall having slalomed down a mountain at 70 m.p.h. but can't remember their skis having actually touched the snow. Marathon runners have experienced coming to the finish line of the 26-mile, 385-yard race and intellectually knowing that crowds of people are lined up on both sides of them only a few feet away but sensing that the people are miles to the side, that their voices are drifting in space from miles away. All of these distortions come from mental focus and the blocking out of outside stimuli, and as John Lilly suggested, the result is extremely productive.

Tennis, football, skiing and running are not cases of strict sensory deprivation, however. In these sports, the athlete blocks out some outside stimulation through intense focus —according to Lilly, the first step in sensory deprivation technique. But the sensory functions, such as vision and hearing, are necessary to perform well in these activities, which makes absolute sensory deprivation impossible. Marathon swimming, on the other hand, is the one sport where an absolute study of sensory deprivation can be made. It is the nature of the sport that the sensory functions cease to operate. It is also the nature of the sport that it lends itself to immediate and extreme self-hypnosis. Marathon swimming produces the same effects as floating in a sensory deprivation tank and magnifies them a hundredfold. After all, there is the added measure of exhaustion that contributes to delirium and to letting the mind loose on its own.

I wear a pair of plastic goggles and try very hard not to touch them for the duration of the swim. I don't want to cover them with grease, and if I secure a proper fit in the beginning, I don't want to take the time and energy later to find that fit again. I have had severe blood clotting in one eye when I swam twenty-four hours in a debris-filled lake without goggles; and one swimmer was permanently blinded after swimming the English Channel without goggles. Even a minor leak can cause great damage. After my first unsuccessful try at Manhattan Island, I had a nasty viral infection I am convinced I caught from water that leaked through my goggles into the tear ducts.

The goggles fog over within just a few minutes after the start of the swim. I am breathing to my left, sixty times a minute, trying to catch a glimpse of my boat and occasionally my trainer through this seemingly dense fog. During the first few hours, when I am fresh, I can read short messages on the blackboard, and for a few hours after that, I can't read words but I can see the large numbers that tell me what hour I'm in. Fatigue and the process of turning the head so many times a minute without ever focusing take their toll, and after approximately ten hours, I become almost blind. The only solution would be to take the goggles off, but my sight would still be extremely poor due to distortion, an experience much like what happens if you step out into the daylight after being enclosed in a pitch-black room for a number of hours. When I can no longer see while swimming, my trainer communicates with me by whistle. If I hear one long pull on the police whistle, I know I am veering too far to the right and I edge back toward the left. Two long pulls means I must edge back toward the right; I am getting too close to the boat. Several short trills mean that I should stop and look to the boat for instruction. I may have swum too far ahead of the boat or am too far behind it; sometimes I am about to run into a dangerous piece of wood or debris, or it is time to approach the boat for a feeding.

My hearing doesn't go completely, but it is 90 percent ineffectual. I can usually hear the police whistle, although the crew often have to give me the signal a dozen times before I hear it and respond accordingly. Well into the swim, it is virtually impossible for me to discern words. If instruction is imperative, I try to raise the caps over my ears; the trainer has to yell at the top of his lungs, slowly and distinctly, and even then I am liable to catch only a couple of words. On the Lake Ontario swim we hooked up giant speakers in hopes that I would be able to hear some music and ease my boredom through the hours. After a few hours the crew had almost gone crazy because the blare was so deafening. I never heard a note.

Because of visual and aural deprivation, all communication is cut off. No outside stimulation can penetrate to the swimmer. Besides sight and hearing, other senses fail. The tactile sense is distorted because of the immersion time. Taste and smell are obliterated in the water. When I am in the middle of the swim, I would give anything for some outside stimulation of any sort. But when the swim is finally over, I realize that the fascinating mental process and the mental exhilaration would never have surfaced without the sensory deprivation.

To me, the long swims have become hypnotic sessions, deprivation tank experiences, LSD trips. My memory delves back into my childhood, to even as early as two years old, to sift through events and reinterpret dialogue that I couldn't possibly remember when "conscious." My imagination flowers to the point that I am wonderfully entertained by the scenes I paint on my eyelids and I am sincerely frightened by the horrors I imagine myself to be confronting. In a swim in the ocean near Argentina I stopped dead in the water, started screaming bloody murder, threw my cap and goggles off, and waved my arms frantically around my head. I thought a pack of gulls, à la Hitchcock, were attacking me and in fact were devouring me. I imagined their beaks gouging my head; the hair was flying off in the wind, the blood was gushing down my face into my eyes. I continued in this fantasy for over half an hour, and to me at that moment, it was a very real, frightening situation.

This is the point when a trainer is crucial. The trainer is concerned with more than your physical well-being, with feeding you and helping prod you to continue. He or she is also in charge of your mental well-being. Before the swim begins, there is a mass meeting of all the swimmer's crew and the captain's crew together. One important subject of the meeting is deciding who is finally in charge of determining whether the swimmer should be taken out of the water or not. Is it the captain, who knows the conditions of the sea? Is it the trainer, who knows the swimmer best? Is it a joint decision of everyone involved?

In my case, I leave this final decision to my head trainer

alone. I am certainly not capable of making any decisions whatsoever, even as to my own well-being; my perceptions of what I am going through have nothing to do with reality. My head trainer, then, must be someone who can judge whether my condition at any point will bring me any permanent physical or mental harm. For instance, the trainer in charge of the English Channel swim in which the man swam without goggles and was blinded should have insisted that the swimmer come out of the water. And there are trainers who, seeing their swimmers in physical pain and extreme discomfort, do them a disservice by taking them out when with a little encouragement they could have gone on. But when the trainer sees his swimmer's eyes go dull and gray or sees him swimming around in tiny circles, it is his duty to recognize that the situation is a dangerous one and that some damage to the mind might ensue if the swimmer's brain is not allowed to withdraw and rest. When I was in the throes of fighting off the gulls, my trainer came close by me in the boat and made a decision. He decided to try to draw me out of the fantasy by entering it with me; and he also decided that if I continued for more than forty-five minutes with no sign of breaking back to reality, he would take me out. He took an oar from the boat and whooshed it over my head for fifteen minutes, swearing at the gulls, screaming for them to get away from me. When I finally abandoned the fantasy and remembered what I was supposed to be doing, he determined that it was safe for me to continue.

In most sports, it isn't easy to reach that point of pure focus where all outside stimulation is blocked out. It isn't easy to self-hypnotize and drift away so that the body can act freely and intuitively as you have devotedly taught it, without interference from the conscious mind. For me, it is so easy to drift light-years away from the conscious world that it often becomes dangerous. Just as a tennis player's swing becomes automatic, my stroke has become automatic. From the first stroke to the last, I never have to think "make the hand entry directly over the shoulder, keep the elbows up, finish the stroke at the thigh, recover with the elbows high." If I'm completely cut off from any outside communication, if I don't have to think about swimming technique, if I'm not capable of focusing on any concrete subject (such as money) for more than thirty seconds, then how is my mind going to occupy itself? Left with such freedom, as on an acid trip, the mind does not restrict itself. Unlike an acid trip, there is no danger of drug abuse to the body and there would seemingly be no reason to stop the mind from going just as far as it wanted. The ideal situation, if letting the mind go were the sole interest, would be to swim for forty hours at a good pace with no athletic objective, no one to beat, no record to break, no record to establish. It would be a much greater mind trip than floating in the deprivation tank, self-hypnosis or meditation. I have done all three; the mind will take a longer and richer voyage during a long swim. On the other hand, it seems so impractical to train like a bastard for years to be able to swim nonstop in open water for forty hours so that you can have a wild mind trip. I have compromised by setting athletic goals for myself while still being able to take the mind trip; the compromise is that I've had to come up with some technique to control the mind expansion so that I won't go too far away and render myself incapable of continuing to swim.

At first I tried singing songs to myself. Popular songs. Beatles. Laura Nyro. But most of the time I was too delirious to remember the exact lyrics or to remember if I had sung one line twice or forgotten a line. And since the songs varied in cadence and rhythm, I was disturbed at not being able to syncopate my stroke with the song. Then I tried making up conversations between people, like I do at home. I would have party A speaking among parties B, C and D in an elaborate discussion about the beginning of the universe. Needless to say, this technique only contributed to my fantasy world instead of serving its intended purpose, which was to keep me in touch with reality as much as possible.

Counting was the answer. I made up counting goals, all of which would ideally correspond to an hour of swimming. I could then come in for the feeding and start back swimming with a new counting goal in mind. Six hundred strokes. A hundred and fifty "Row, Row, Row Your Boat"s. Twenty-five "Frère Jacques"s in sets of French, German and English. Ad infinitum. The counting acts as a hypnotic device in that the rhythmic counting over the hours lets the mind relax and dip further into fantasy. And the counting keeps my inner voice busy with some intelligible, conscious-world symbols so that I'm not so far gone as to be out of control. The counting helps me float in limbo between the unbearable sanity of knowing the exact extent of the pain I am feeling and the glorious insanity of zooming away on a wild, safe LSD trip.

Floating in the tank, undergoing self-hypnosis, and meditating have two effects in common with long-distance swimming. First, they set the mind free of conscious, sensory, social demands and allow it to explore with no attachments. Second, the individual feels rested after the session. But "rested" is not precisely the word to describe the marathon swimmer at the other shore. "Comatose" would perhaps be better. Although if the physical can ever be clearly separated from the mental, I can say that I am mentally rested, almost relieved, after a long swim. Of course, the brain needs rest because it hasn't slept for so many hours and it is also fatigued from the moments of conscious concentration when a quick trip back to full reality was needed. On the other hand, I always say that the experience of doing a marathon swim is like spending six months on a shrink's couch. Due to the exhaustion and the hypnotic counting and stroking and the sensory deprivation effects, you have remembered so much and imagined so much and discovered so much about yourself and others that the whole psychological experience is very rich, rewarding and calming. Each decade of life usually brings with it more calm, more assurance of who you are and what you want. Each marathon swim seems to make you psychologically a decade older.

I don't mean to imply that the marathon swim is a pleasurable mental experience as it is happening. The physical difficulties of the marathon prevent the mind expansion during the swim from being pure pleasure. The pleasure of the mind trip is a cumulative phenomenon. It presents itself as an after-effect when the extremity of the physical stress is over.

I also don't mean to imply that every marathon swimmer derives the same psychological benefits and pleasures from the long swim. As a matter of fact, during my career as a marathoner, I have known only one man who can relate to my sensations and share his own similar experiences with me. He is Raul Villagomez from Mexico. (I am sure it is telling that out of the water I also relate to Raul better than to any of the other marathoners.) The sport doesn't guarantee mind trips and discoveries, but it is conducive to such trips if the individual is open and willing. After a fairly long swim in Europe during the early seventies, I asked a Dutch swimmer friend of mine what he had been thinking about at certain points in the race. He said that during the fifth hour he was thinking that he had to win because his wife was pregnant and they needed the money. During the seventh hour he was thinking that he had to beat one of the other Dutch swimmers because his reputation in the home press was slipping. And during the thirteenth hour he remembered thinking that he was mad at himself for not having kicked more before the race because his legs were terribly tired. I asked him if he had fantasized at all, imagined any scenes or re-created any moments from the past. He answered no, that he hadn't remembered thinking anything like that.

It seems that I bring something to the sport, just as it brings something to me—a marriage made in heaven. Beside the sensory deprivation and the mental maturity and exhilaration marathon swimming provides, it led to my interest in dream therapy, another subject I experimented with for two years.

It was fascinating to me that I could break world records while immersed in such a consuming fantasy world. After a couple of years on the pro circuit I began to notice a correlation between the two; my best races were those in which my fantasies were rich, intense and long-lasting. But how was it possible? How could my mind be in outer space, having forgotten who I was or what I was doing, while my body was stroking away at a world-class pace? Sometimes the screeching police whistle would shock me out of my dream world and I would be utterly amazed to discover that I was in the middle of some lake or ocean next to a boatload of frantic voices. As the brain quickly shifted back to the real world, I would be even more amazed to learn that I had swum another hour, it was time for another feeding, and I had moved up three positions in the race. I thought this was the unique case of marathon swimming where being alert was not a prerequisite to success. But I found that the trick of taking the mind elsewhere to let the body perform without conscious interference was used with great results in other activities where sensory alertness is imperative. It's the step directly after pinpoint focus.

If the tennis players, football players, skiers and runners who have superior concentration in blocking out all outside stimuli could take that next step toward separating the intellectual and the intuitive, they would be better yet. And some of them do. Billie Jean King, whom I believe has an extraordinary ability to tune into the ball while tuning everything else out, has said that the time distortion during a match is occasionally very severe. A set of forty minutes may seem to take only five minutes. As I do in marathon swimming, she lets the intellect take a trip while the intuitive plays tennis.

And there are anecdotes from other fields that illustrate the same point. For instance, in his book *Powers of Mind*, Adam Smith reports asking Jascha Heifetz what he thought about while giving a concert. Heifetz answered that, as an example, if the concert were on a Saturday night, he would think about the bagel he would have for breakfast the next day. Yet another story involves an American lawyer, who in 1972 owned 100 percent of the shares of a small food chain. He decided to cash in on his original investment, which had been small, and he sold his shares for nearly a million dollars. He was elated with his business brilliance and returned to his law practice a rich man. By 1975, that food chain had grown into a multimillion-dollar business. True to the Wall

Street ethic, the businessman was no longer happy with what he had made; he was extremely depressed in thinking of what he could have made and didn't. Clinically depressed, he gradually became incapable of working, his wife left him and he twice attempted suicide. Friends persuaded him to seek professional help, and after monthly trials with psychiatrists, drugs, meditation gurus and so forth, he found hypnosis to be a great relief. He would readily go under and come out feeling somewhat rested and relaxed. After several months he'd made a lot of progress: he'd begun to work again and to straighten out his personal life, and he continued to see his hypnosis therapist once a week. He also hypnotized himself once a day, or more often if he felt tense or pressured. If he was at his office, he would ask his secretary not to bother him for forty-five minutes; he would stare at a point on the ceiling, go under for a while and wake up feeling able to cope. The interesting note is that he began to do the best work of the day while under hypnosis. He would wake up to discover that he had written a brilliant letter, or negotiated a contractual point on the phone or done something better than he felt he could have done when "straight." These were things that he had been trained to do and had practiced for many years, just as a superior tennis player has practiced the aspects of that trade for many years, just as Heifetz has practiced the violin for many years. Sports are not the only field where separating the intellect from intuition can be productive.

It is said that the human uses approximately 12 percent of the brain's capacity. It is assumed that as we evolve further, we will use a larger and larger percentage. But why wait for evolution? Neurologists and neurophysiologists aren't entirely sure as to the possible potential of each section of the brain. As a matter of fact, they are not entirely sure which sections of the brain are responsible for the functions we already command. I collect articles on the brain from the *Journal of the American Medical Association* and other publications, and there seems to be only one sure fact—the more we discover about the brain, the more we are convinced what a complex, mysterious creature it is. A general theory that has been suggested for centuries is that the left side of the cerebral cortex is responsible for concrete, verbal, rational behavior while the right side controls abstract, conceptual behavior. Intellect versus intuition. Narcissus versus Goldmund. And "versus" is precisely right. It seems that we are not very successful in working both sides simultaneously. If the left side is active balancing a complicated mathematical equation, the right side is basically dormant; if the right side is busy choreographing a ballet, the left side takes a nap.

These are blatantly layman's terms; the process is much more complicated. I had a theory, however, that stemmed from this idea of the right side resting while the left side worked and vice versa. It seemed that if you could get them to operate simultaneously more often, you would tap a greater percentage of the brain's potential and you might experience a unique sensation. After all, I believe this is what happens during a marathon swim. You are somewhere in limbo between the absolute concrete world of conscious thought and the seemingly uncontrollable state of illogical fantasy. The result is a phenomenal mind expansion.

Outside marathon swimming, during a normal day, I felt that my brain's activities were divided into two parts and that they generally did not share time. During the waking hours, my left side would communicate with written and spoken language, would research graduate school papers, would negotiate the money end of a contract. The right side would sleep. During the sleeping hours, the right side would produce images, colors, movements, scenes, for continuous hours while the left side rested from the day's activity. My intention wasn't to get the left side to function while sleeping. It can be done, but I believe that the left side needs a few hours of complete rest every day. (I studied German, which is a left-side duty, by playing tapes during my sleep, and although I did increase my learning pace, I was constantly tired the next day as if I hadn't had a good enough sleep.) I wanted to give the left side a rest; my idea was to draw the right side out during the waking hours. I thought if I could get that process of night dreaming (not daydreaming where you have control over your fantasy) to operate when I was awake, I would enjoy the rich mental activity of the long swims.

I began a hypnotic technique experiment that changed forms many times. In its most successful stage, I would play tapes all through my sleeping hours. These were all tapes I had made with my own voice. They weren't of an intellectual nature, so the left side was not awakened. Most of them were series of counting such as I use on the swims; a few had recordings of Mozart or Chopin with which I was very familiar. If, for example, I was going to sleep six hours, I set six different tapes in six different machines hooked up to timers so that the second tape would click on automatically as the first one played out its sixty minutes. (I found that using one tape over and over again for six hours, although easier mechanically, had little effect. The brain seems to get used to repetitive sounds and ceases to listen.)

The theory behind the tapes was that I would slip into a deeper REM sleep and dream more throughout the night. So the first result was giving the left side deeper and better-quality rest. The second result, as I had hoped, was that I would remember these dreams during the following day; the counting on the tapes allowed me to dream more and helped me remember my dreams. Not just as I woke up in the morning, but throughout the waking day I would flash back to entire dreams from the previous night. And like the delirious fantasies of the swims, these dreams were filled with childhood memories I could never have dug up consciously, strange combinations of people I knew and fictional characters, remarkably creative dialogue. I was not in the least interested in interpreting my dreams. My goal was to experience right-side activity openly during the waking hours to enrich the left side's point of view. For a period of almost one and a half years, I was consistently recalling forty full dreams every day, which was very exciting and very bizarre. I was not attempting to suppress left-side activity during the waking hours. As Carl Sagan suggests in *The Dragons of Eden*, humans have probably come as far as they have by giving the "reptilian brain" less time while developing the left-lobe potential. I wanted the left lobe and the right lobe, the intellectual and the creative, to work simultaneously more often than they did.

Eventually the experiment tapered off. I suffered a traumatic emotional experience that affected my deep sleep ability, so I gave up the tapes for a while. Also, I noticed that the number of recalled dreams had begun to diminish even before that. I suppose the brain began to tune out the tapes it had heard so many times. In any case, even though I have absolutely no scientific expertise, I felt the experiment was successful. I experienced the intellectual and the intuitive, the rational and the irrational, the concrete and the abstract simultaneously, without the use of drugs. And without a marathon swim.

7. The English Channel

~~~~~~

AUGUST 5, 1976. I was wedged into one of British Airway's economy seats, happily accompanied by my two closest friends, who were to act as my trainers, and by an American film crew of seven. We were off to make, assist and record history. I was attempting to become the first woman to complete the double crossing of the English Channel. The swim would be from shore to shore, followed by the permissible ten minutes' rest, and then back again. This was to be one of my toughest moments, and as the date was set for August 15, I had ten days to gather all my assets to a pinpoint focus on the Channel.

It was a night flight; I've always admired people who could sleep sitting up, but I'm not among them, so I dug into the corner of an Adidas bag for Channel swimming literature. *The Channel Swimming Association Handbook* was a bit dry. The list of attempts, successes and records was better; to date only 20 percent of the 1,100 who had attempted the crossing had succeeded. Then I settled down to hundreds of anecdotes of Channel swims, successes as well as failures. Filled with heroism, human drama and fascinating detail, these pages aroused in me once again a tremendous appreciation for this sport, which embraces so much more than the perfecting of specified skills and the mental/physical battle with an opponent. Engrossed by the stories, I also wondered at the fact that, while the English Channel is reputed the world round as the greatest long-distance swimming test, very few people know who has done it or what it involves (except, of course, the enthusiastic and knowledgeable inhabitants of the English coast, who say that had it been dubbed the "French Channel," the interest would have been generated on the other shore).

Who knows the story of Captain Matthew Webb, considered the laughable lunatic of London, who in 1875 set off covered with porpoise oil, with little navigational expertise, slow breast-stroking at one mile per hour, gulping brandy for warmth? Webb was the first to swim across (England to France, 21 hours, 45 minutes), and at the time, his feat was looked upon by those who hadn't actually been witnesses in much the same way as centenarians today view astronauts walking on the moon—pure fiction. (Some weeks later Webb tried to cross the Niagara River four hundred meters above the falls; he is buried at the bottom.) Then there was the man who had been close to losing consciousness an hour from shore, but as he slowly approached the English coast a large wave threw him onto the rocks, at which point he did lose consciousness; as he slipped back into the sea, the next roller tossed him farther than the first, and he thereby completed the swim. And there was barrel-chested Kevin Murphy, who went looking for the first-ever three-way crossing (over, back and over again). One year (1974) he started twelve hours too late: at the fifty-second hour, on his way to the third coast, tremendous winds blew up, forcing him to abandon the effort. Then in July 1976, he began twelve hours too soon, as the light west wind, which switched to an easterly twelve hours after he started, blew diesel fumes straight in his face, inducing many hours of vomiting that reduced him to hopeless exhaustion. And there are scores of stories told of severe jellyfish stings, the famed Channel chop that always seems to come up against you, the icy temperatures, the abrupt changes in weather, different pilots' theories about courses and their almost intuitive interpretation of the tides and wind-force readings.

After a short train ride from London, we checked into the stately White Cliffs Hotel on the harbor front in Dover. One hour later, staring out toward France from my balcony, brimming with fear and excitement, I began to prepare myself.

Swimming has always deserved its reputation as one of the tough sports, the time-consuming sports in which long hours of conditioning can't be avoided. No swimmer arrives at the English Channel or at any other body of water without months and months of strenuous interval training in a pool, monotonous rhythmic hours in open water, and a few long solo crossings under his or her belt. And although I knew the difficulty of conquering the Channel to be highly overrated, despite its public acclaim, my discipline in training for the double crossing hadn't been lax in any way. During the previous five months I had completed three swims of eight, twelve and thirteen hours; and I had put in a hell of a lot of time at the pool, all building toward an intense month of July. Mondays, Wednesdays and Fridays I did ten miles; eight on Tuesdays and Thursdays; and weekends I would go out for open-water swims in the cold waters of the New York area, off Long Island and Fire Island. August meant a welcome tapering, two weeks of light training, loosening up, massages, overresting—and overeating. Except for my weight, I was in perfect physical shape. At 125 pounds, 5 feet 6 1/2 inches, I then had nine days to pump up to what I thought would be an ideal weight of 140. (The very cold Channel temperature—it reads approximately 58 degrees during the summer season—burns up a lot of calories.) No coat of porpoise oil or lanolin can contain body heat and maintain body temperature as well as fatty tissue. Moreover, the caloric output of a marathon swimmer at a decent pace in cold water is from 1,500 to 2,500 calories per hour; and although you feed on liquids rich in glucose while swimming, the calories lost couldn't possibly be reingested fast enough to hold a constant weight. So the prime source of energy becomes the body fat itself.

Gaining weight became one preoccupation. Another was the logistics of the crossing. Through the Channel Swimming Association, the body of officials that organizes, sanctions and records Channel swims, I had prearranged to be piloted by a veteran Channel fisherman named Heath. If most of the stories told could be believed, success was often as dependent on the boat captain as on the swimmer. Evidently, an experienced and interested pilot could guide even the poorest of swimmers across, whereas the best of swimmers could be thwarted in crossing attempts by the inept navigation and bad judgment of an inexperienced one. I was most anxious to meet this Heath.

We took a bus to the next town, wound our way through the cobblestone streets to the wharves and pounded on Heath's door. It opened shortly, a voice with a very strong accent announced "Auwt beck," and the door was shut again. We traipsed around to the back to find Heath, an almost archetypical old salt, toothless and quiet, with most of his eleven children on the lawn nearby. Introductions went around; my group and his group stepped aside and we held our first meeting, Heath and I, standing arms folded amidst the laundry hanging in his backyard. I trusted him implicitly.

We first discussed the tides. The spring (strong) tides occur every fortnight, three days after the new moon or the full moon. The springs run five to six times faster than a swimmer's speed and are often so strong that breaking in toward shore for landing becomes impossible. Neap (slack) tides also occur every fortnight, three days after the first and last quarters of the moon. Even though the three-to-four-knot strength of the neaps is still faster than average swimming speed for any length of time, a swim, and especially a double crossing, is more easily and safely accomplished during this period. The next neaps were to run from August 17 to 23. The August 15 date I had been given was correct because the tides begin to slacken a couple of days before the neaps actually run.

I was to be second in line with Heath for the mid-August neaps. There would be an all-Arab race on the 15th, weather permitting; he was committed to one of the competitors, and he would then be available to escort me, weather permitting. Weather permitting? Every race I had been to was sent off in any conditions short of a hurricane. Here the wind is measured by the Beaufort scale of wind forces 0 through 17: force 0, up to one mile per hour; force 4, whitecaps are forming; force 7, a gale; and forces 12 to 17, a hurricane. The weather is so unpredictable through the

Dover Straits that Coast Guard and shipping forecasts are secured only twelve hours in advance and nobody promises anything. The captain listens for a force 0 to 1, 1 to 2, 2 to 3 or possibly 3 to 4 (if the wind is behind you), and you take off on the next tide, some eleven hours later. Can you imagine showing up at Wimbledon, thoroughly prepared for your moment, only to discover that nobody knows whether you will play the night of the 15th or the afternoon of the 16th; perhaps you will even have to bide your time and hold your peak until the early morning of the 24th, still with no more than twelve hours' notice? If the task of preparation is to peak at a distinct moment, how thorough will the preparation ever be when the moment is so indistinct as to be left in the laps of the Channel weather gods?

The next week's routine was to become one of frustrating but beneficial boredom. Swimming, sleeping and eating. Mostly eating. Sumptuous breakfasts, several light meals during the day, Cadbury chocolate by the pound, dozens of baked potatoes and ears of corn, two or three desserts at dinner. As the Arabs were to compete on the 15th, I thought my starting time would likely be 3:00 A.M. on August 16. I put myself on a descending training schedule: the first few days entailed swimming a few hours and the time spent decreased each day until it was only a matter of thirty to forty-five minutes of relaxed stretching. The sleeping/resting was a system I call overloading. After many months of hard work you reach a point in conditioning that defies fatigue. A tapering period allows for full recovery and sharpening of the edge; and overloading on rest for five or six days before a marathon swim conserves energy and adrenaline until you feel you could explode. Beginning August 12, most of my time was spent quietly, generating the presence of mind to expect the worst and to handle the worst, this time perhaps for a continuous thirty hours. By the 15th I was sky-high and ready, weighing a strong 139 pounds, bursting with confidence and ambition. My head was willing to permit my body any and every abuse.

But the Arab race never set off on the 15th. Or the 16th. Or the 17th. They finally had a chance the morning of the 18th, so I knew my moment would come the following day. Apprehensive about the delay, not having swum for five days, perhaps not as thoroughly peaked as the few days before, I was up again. The film crew was to be on the pilot's boat in the harbor at 9:00 A.M. They would taxi over to Shakespeare Beach, where my trainers would be greasing me. Departure time was set for 10:30, one hour after high water. I downed as many carbohydrates as humanly possible throughout the day—spaghetti, toast and honey, bowls of cereal, baked potatoes. I soaked in a hot bath, tried to relax with a full massage and had ten hours of uneasy sleep. At 7:30 A.M. I was dressing for the preswim meal when the phone rang. Heath—bad weather. Christ, off again. This procedure was to continue in much the same fashion for the following four days. An afternoon forecast at 2:00 would give a tentative go-ahead for the next day, the 6:00 P.M. report would boost my hopes further, but then Heath's call would come through in the morning, canceling day after day, chance after chance. Indefatigable faith began to waver and the physical peak was definitely slipping from its solid groundwork. You can't entirely forgo swimming for ten or twelve—or who knows how many—days before the chance comes; but you can't swim much either, because you may be alerted that you're going off in a few hours and every ounce of reserve will be needed. After passing days and weeks in frustrated waiting, countless swimmers have done a decent training swim in an effort to regain both a mental and physical edge, only to learn the weather has changed and they are scheduled to go that evening at midnight.

August 23 came and went, the last day of the neaps. The film people were anxious, to say the least; this was a hell of an investment and a hell of a risk if no swim was to materialize. I was a nervous wreck, no longer assuring myself how well I would attack the task but wondering if the task would ever offer itself. It did—the next day.

The spring tide beginning to roll, the wind coming at force 2 to 3 from the east, August 24 wouldn't present the glassy mirror of all swimmers' daydreams, but it was an opportunity nonetheless, and we marched determinedly down Shakespeare Beach after the customary ritual of much food and little sleep. With the understandable fear in the back of my mind that the whole thing would be called off at the last minute, I was pensive and took a few minutes for my final meditation. Heath contacted us from the boat on the two-way radio—the swim was on. I was to be greased and waiting for the observer's signal at 1:00 A.M. (An observer is provided by the Channel Swimming Association to officiate a swim, to clock the exact time, and no swim is recognized without one.) I pulled down my suit, and with the aid of an onlooker's flashlight, my two trainers began greasing my torso. It is a singular feeling to stand naked below the towering Shakespeare Cliff in the middle of a cool English night and sense the rubber gloves slapping pounds and pounds of thick grease on your smooth skin. My concoction was 90 percent lanolin, 10 percent paraffin. Some swimmers add silicone fluid as a water repellent; some of the heavier ones have used axle grease; some stick to wool fat, or lanolin by itself; and some go with only Vaseline. If the truth were known, except for the prevention of chafing at the neck, under the arms and between the legs, there isn't a grease made that will serve its intended purpose of keeping in the warmth, keeping out the cold. For me it has become a psychological crutch to know that before a cold-water swim I will start off with six extra pounds of blubber, even though the bulk of it thins and washes off within the first hour.

Heath's boat came within sight at 12:45 A.M.; a rubber inflatable was sent in for the trainers and cameraman; the observer gave the arm signal to begin at 1:03. I stumbled over the rocks at the water's edge, slipped into the cool sea and began stroking. I remembered all the preparations I had made for the thirty-hour swim. I thought of the quick feedings every hour on the hour that would be goals in themselves. I focused on the format of chants and songs I had organized to preoccupy myself during each hour—numbers to count, numbers to reach by the feeding. This hypnotic technique was designed to keep my concentration intact for as long as possible; the isolation and the monotony and the extreme fatigue all seem to eat away at mental control, and when the mental control goes, the will goes and you're through.

From the onset to the first feeding I counted strokes, or each time the left hand entered the water. Eighteen hundred strokes was the goal. The wind coming from the east and my head turning to breathe in almost the same direction meant that I occasionally swallowed water. But during the first hour there were far too many gulps. Stroking 1,797, 1,798, 1,799, 1,800, 1,801—the trainer's whistle and feeding time. I veered toward the boat, gradually approached the starboard, and reached up for the cup, which was extended to me in a small pan attached to a wooden pole. I would fish into the pan, grab the cup and down the twelve ounces of hot Sustagen (a hot chocolate with tremendous protein, salt, mineral and glucose levels) in less than twenty seconds.

Tossing the cup to the wind, turning again toward France, I began the second hour's counting, the goal being to hit 225 complete "Row, Row, Row Your Boat"s before the feeding whistle. Only seconds later I vomited heavily, losing the benefit of the first feeding, and as the end of the second hour approached, I was in deep trouble. "Row, row, row . . . life is but a dream," 220, " . . . life is but a dream," 221, the whistle. I took the second cup of chocolate and began vomiting and dry-heaving for twenty minutes, treading water, knowing I couldn't even touch the boat for support. The fifteen people on the boat became alarmed; they tried to communicate with me, tried to suggest ways to combat the nausea. Panic also stirred in my heart—the end was near.

Within minutes I was lying on the deck, wrapped in blankets. Voices at once barraged me with sympathy. Never mind, just bad luck; the Sustagen was too rich to mix with salt water; not such a great day anyway. But I closed my eyes and cried tears for the death of a love that was once the core of my universe. I had swum all over the world with the added pressure of racing world-caliber athletes instead of going it solo. I had held world records across the cold Canadian lakes, from Capri to Naples, down the Argentinian rivers and the Nile. I had held the male and female records for both the north-south crossing of Lake Ontario (18 hours, 20 minutes) and the circling of Manhattan Island (7 hours, 57 minutes). Marathon swimming had once offered me the

pinnacle of an exhilarating mental/physical/emotional challenge, and now I was faced with the harsh realization that
the horizons were no longer wide enough, that the love affair
was fading.

My moment of soul-searching had arrived, I suppose, and
as our boat slowly puffed back to England and waited two
hours to clear immigration, I was enormously depressed.
After we docked, we loaded our van and squeezed in; no one
spoke as we drove the fifteen minutes back to the hotel.
Weary, still swaying and still silent, we dragged ourselves
into the foyer, and I solemnly asked if we could all meet for
one minute. Everyone pulled up chairs and waited with tired
but respectful eyes. I was filled with emotion. Enveloped in
greasy blankets, looking from face to face, I spoke slowly and
softly. After seven hard years at the top of one of the most
difficult sports, I sincerely appreciated the fact that the
members of this film company were the first people to believe in what I did, to invest money on the faith that a visual
record of what I did would be valuable. (I made more money
attempting the English Channel than I did in six years of
professional marathon swimming.) They had spent a lot of
time and money, my good friends had lent their time and
energy, and I was sorry. Almost feeling guilty, I told them
that seasickness didn't induce my defeat. I had been seasick
a dozen times before, and seasickness doesn't make a champion quit. I said that although physical strength, a fine pilot,
efficient trainers, blood sugar replacement and so forth all
help you across, only your motivation will actually get you
there. If you want to touch the other shore badly enough,
barring an impossible situation, you will. If your desire is
diluted for any reason, you'll never make it. I said I was like
a fighter who was still good, who still made the right moves

and who still enjoyed being called the champ, but who just didn't want to take any more punches. The thrill wasn't what it used to be; it had been fading for a couple of years, and if a thrill is no more than a memory, however wonderful, it has no place in the present. I regretted that I had to discover this truth now instead of a month earlier, when I could have analyzed my feelings at home. But I supposed it could have only been discovered swimming again, seeking the thrill again. The group thanked me for sharing my thoughts with them, and we went upstairs.

Dawn broke. I took a bath and swabbed myself with alcohol in another futile attempt to remove the grease. I tried to sleep, but I was anxious, my heart was heavy. I had failed, given up. I had been weak; I hadn't been disciplined enough to make myself do it just because I said I could and would. I felt somehow guilty. Perhaps I had learned a prime lesson for the future—that it was time to move on to something new, but I was still here, there was time to do it right, to leave the old with a grand success instead of a failure.

There were many arguments the next day. Friends said it was a masochistic sport in the first place; wanting to do it again was my intellect speaking, while my words the night before in the foyer came from the heart. Was I really going to do something now that I definitely didn't want to do? I who always bragged that I never, never do anything I don't want to do? Yes, I was. Just this once more and I would go home a winner. And they were with me; the whole crew stayed and believed with me again. The slight change in motivation would make this swim the most difficult of all. It was not the pure desire to win, to finish; it was more the loathing of the self-respect I would lose if I quit.

I asked Heath that night if he would take me again. "Very

good swimmer. Of course I will." He had two Indians—a fourteen-year-old girl and a fifty-four-year-old man—in line starting September 1 for the next neaps, so I would have to wait my turn. And before the neaps? That was up to me, he said meaningfully, so I resolved we'd go the first good day, regardless of the tide. The weather came around on August 30. Heath said there would be some wind, force 4 from the northwest, but it would be blowing from behind, so that was all right. But what about swimming back? I was told I should have learned by then not to ask for everything at the Channel.

August 30 was a retake of August 24. Same breakfast, same people doing the same jobs, same fears and nervousness, and once more confidence and desire. The starting time was now 3:30 A.M. and I was again nude on Shakespeare Beach. Other swimmers set off at approximately the same time; from the first stroke I felt fantastically smooth and powerful. Eighteen hundred strokes, first feeding. Two hundred and nineteen "Row, Row, Row Your Boat"s, second feeding. Thirty-five "Frère Jacques"s (sets of English, French and German), third feeding. I was making splendid headway, I was optimistic and in control, the people on the boat were happy and with me. My only worry was that the seas were beginning to rise; I was thrown about more and more violently and progress was coming to a gradual halt. Two hundred and two "Anything You Can Do, I Can Do Better"s, and I came in for the fourth feeding. Cramps in the left groin from kicking so hard to catch a breath amidst the waves. I knew that the weather was going to beat me this time. Another fifteen or twenty minutes of trying to straighten my left leg, trying to fight the swells, and that was it. The first time I defeated myself; this time I was had by a greater force than anyone could battle. On the boat I learned that the other swimmers were also out. The wind was now at force 6, all the landlubbers had been violently sick and I saw from a better vantage point that the Channel was a mass of breaking whitecaps. There was no guilt or depression this time. August 30 was without a trace of doubt my mental and physical best. Everyone knew it, and we all talked jovially on the way back to shore. The film crew thought that with a statement from me they could salvage something, although it would not be the film they set out to make. They would head back to New York. My two friends and I decided to go to Paris to throw away the rest of our money.

A hot-water bath and an alcohol bath. No sleep. Drunk with sleeplessness, we zoomed down to Paris, talking of things other than swimming. We stayed in a hundred-dollar-a-night hotel, ate on the Champs Élysées, explored Versailles and happily headed home. We waited at the airport, and through some special nonverbal communication we all knew that I was going back to Dover. We embraced, they flew back to the United States, and I would not be defeated by the English Channel.

Still not having slept for some forty-eight hours except for naps on the train, I went straight to Heath. The Indian girl had tried and failed and the Indian man had hurt his back, so I was first in line again. I asked the observer's daughter to be my trainer, found someone willing to grease me on the shore, and set about regathering new gear, this time at my own expense. Grease, thermoses, Dynamo (a glucose drink that seemed to settle with the salt water better than the rich Sustagen), rubber gloves, towels and blankets, biscuits, ginger ale.

I found a wonderful bed-and-breakfast in Dover, checked into an attic room and tried to catch up on some sleep. It was difficult. I was worried, almost desperate to finally tame this Channel and be done with it. I became more and more nervous each day. Heath didn't call when he said he would, the air and water temperatures were beginning to drop, I wasn't sleeping well and I was losing weight. In five days I read *All the President's Men*, *Watership Down*, the murder case of *Mary Bell* and Thor Heyerdahl's *Ra Expeditions*.

On September 5, I called the Coast Guard myself and couldn't believe my ears. Force 1 to 2, westerly, for the early evening, probably continuing through the night and not building up again until midday of the 6th. I was frantic. I would not spend one more restless night and take a chance on the weather changing drastically. I called Heath immediately to tell him I wanted to leave on the 10:30 tide that night. It was 2:00, so there was ample time. The first mate, one of his sons, said that was okay, but to be absolutely sure we should wait for the 6:00 P.M. forecast. They would phone me at 6:10 in any case. My hands were shaking, my head was pounding. I felt tremendous pressure, all self-imposed. I was down to 127 pounds, but I was determined to make this swim. I couldn't sleep, so I stared out the attic window at the white cliffs of France, the first time the weather had permitted me to see them. Though twenty-one miles away, they seemed close enough to touch; the water was like a millpond.

I steeled myself, thought that the third time is the lucky one and went downstairs to wait for the word. They were late in calling, as usual, but this time I became furious. How could they be so inconsiderate as to leave me pacing, worrying, wondering with only four hours to prepare? I called the

Coast Guard, who reconfirmed the earlier forecast: it was to be beautifully calm all night. At 6:40 I called Heath and aggressively told his son I would be on the beach ready to go at 10:30. He interrupted, "No swim tonight. Bad weather." "You're insane!" I screamed, losing control. "The weather couldn't be better!" He said the old man wasn't going. I hung up and stormed outside.

After cooling down I phoned them back. I argued that this was a business arrangement, that I was paying them to do a job and they were obligated to take me. He said the truth of the matter was that old Heath wasn't feeling so well, and he never liked the night swimming anyway. I could barely think, I was so upset and annoyed. I said again that I was going that night, not the next day, and asked if I would have to get another captain in that case. He said he supposed I would.

There was one skipper with a good reputation available, Burt Reed, who said he would be glad to escort me. He agreed that it was a perfect night, so he would do his best to round his crew up, although it was dangerously short notice. I tried to eat a high-calorie meal about three hours before take-off, but it wouldn't stay down. Reed kept calling to report that he hadn't found his crew yet, but it was still not an impossibility. I felt feverish and ill. Finally at 9:00 he called to say we would have to wait for the morning; he had done his best and that was all he could do.

I fixed my eyes on the delicious flat calm, beginning to feel somewhat fatalistic about the whole thing, and spent one last distressed, sleepless night. Two of the film people, having heard that I was back and trying again, returned to help. It was a welcome diversion; I briefed them and we set off at 11:00 the next morning.

A new boat, new pilot, no experienced trainer; nonethe-less, everything was going well. I started on time; the weather was good, although nothing like the night before. During the first hour's counting, I noticed that the water was remarkably colder, and of course my weight loss hadn't helped on that score. First feeding down and I felt fine. Second hour, "Row, Row, Row Your Boat." I began to tremble and just told myself, "It's not so bad, you've been cold before, keep swimming, keep swimming." Third hour, "Frère Jacques." The trembling increased to shaking; I pic-tured the sun at my solar plexus, a Tibetan meditative tech-nique, trying to feel the warmth move to the limbs. Fourth hour, "Anything You Can Do." As I reached for the fourth feeding my hand was shaking too wildly to grasp the cup, so I skipped it. I found out later that everyone on the boat feared for me at that fourth feeding; they told me my skin had been bluish, and they knew that even will power couldn't fight the cold. Fifth hour, "I've Been Working on the Railroad." Chilled to the bone, I was quickly losing touch and my concentration was fading. I couldn't count very well and I kept forgetting what I was doing. I thought birds were dive-bombing my cap and goggles; I frantically waved them away. Suddenly, I heard many long pulls on the police whistle accompanied by frenzied shouting; I stopped to look, and surprised and bewildered, I found the boat on my right instead of my left. How did it get over there without my seeing it? Why were they so upset? They were yelling, but I couldn't hear their words. I don't remember much after that. They say I took another feeding and began swimming again, and about forty-five minutes later I started going under. Evidently, they were to me within seconds. I was hauled into the lifeboat, and as they were transferring me to the fishing vessel, I came to and realized what had happened. My body was jerking uncontrollably; they covered me immediately and two of the crew pressed their bodies to me in an offer of the best heat available. One of the mates got some hot bouillon down my throat, and within an hour the trembling began to subside. The captain kneeled beside me and comforted me with a warm hand and large smiling blue eyes. He said I was a good swimmer—I had done ten miles into mid-Channel in a bit more than four hours; I would have reached France in a very short time, indeed; if I put some weight on, I was sure to have a good crack at the record next time; he would be only too pleased to escort me on that occasion; yes, he would.

Unfortunately, the Channel was not a glorious success to be tallied up for the record along with my many other crossings. It was a defeat. Once I weakened mentally, once the weather wouldn't permit success, and ironically, the villain I had originally feared and had set out to vanquish— the cold—was my ultimate downfall. I realized that it is mechanically so easy to walk away from victory swelling with pride and optimism, believing unswervingly in yourself. Walking away from defeat the same way is a true challenge. A champion rekindles enthusiasm, regains confidence, and is willing to set difficult goals for herself again, even after defeat.

Late evening, September 7. British Airways from London to Kennedy. My pulse is racing, my adrenaline is pumping, I am smiling uncontrollably and I can't possibly sit still. Push-ups in the aisle, hyped conversation with anyone and everyone. I feel ecstatically free. The words I am known for quoting to interviewers are flashing through my mind. Life is passing me by. There isn't much time. I have some seventy-five years to live and a third of them are behind me. I feel pressured to do everything, to know everyone, to explore every potential, to press every extreme, high and low. My fervor is renewed.

8. Why?

~~~~~~

Sleepe after toyle, port after stormie seas,
Ease after warre, death after life, does greatly please.
—EDMUND SPENSER, *The Faerie Queene*

MARATHON SWIMMING is the most boring and the most
fascinating sport in the world. The endless, seemingly tireless lifting of arm after arm, hour after hour, means no
change, no spontaneity. No one wants to watch a swimmer
stroke sixty times a minute, six hundred times an hour, for
ten, twenty, thirty, forty, fifty hours. Yet hundreds of thousands will wait many hours themselves to witness the swimmer's exhausted emergence on the other shore. As in the
Tour de France, where almost the entire French population
gathers in the little towns at night to catch a fleeting glimpse
of those completely spent forms hunched in pain over their
bicycles, people wait on the shores of oceans, lakes and rivers
all over the world to stand in awe of a person who has just
triumphed over a host of seemingly insurmountable difficul-

ties. Interviewers ask in a perplexed tone what it feels like to be chilled to the bone in the water for a full twenty-four hours. Strangers seem perversely intrigued by someone swimming fourteen hours while being seasick every ten or fifteen minutes. Friends want to know how one copes with the delirium for such a long time. Everyone is curious, everyone is respectful, and everyone seeks a response to the same question. Why?

Point-blank, there is no logic to it. It is reason enough that I have done swims and that I continue to do swims. As Amelia Earhart said, "I want to do it because I want to do it." The why is complex, but the core of an explanation lies in one word: extremity. What interests me about marathon swimming is that it tests the human spirit. It is a sport of extremes. The real issue behind reaching the other shore is neither talent nor preparation nor the outwitting of an opponent. The real issue is the strength of the human will and the ability to focus that will under the most unimaginable of circumstances.

Since adolescence, I have become a quasi-authority on survival stories—stories about people who are pushed beyond every conceivable recourse—and I realize that the attraction lies in the extremity. Survival is the extreme moment of everyday life as marathon swimming is the extreme moment of sport. And although one is never in direct peril of losing one's life during a long swim (good friends disagree with me here), many of the stages of a marathon swim correlate closely with the stages of survival.

Probably the most devastating survival stories during the era of modern man are those of the Nazi concentration camp prisoners. The words of the survivors of Auschwitz, Buchenwald and the Russian camps resound with the purest testimony to the subtle yet relentless life force that is the human will. These people were inescapably immersed in an environment bent on eradicating their dignity, their sense of self. Time was no longer meaningful; every minute of every day seemed precisely the same. There was no goal or purpose; after all, they had no idea how long the ordeal would go on. The values of civilized life no longer counted; intelligence, experience, education, cunning were insignificant. Every moment hinged on the basics: food, air, excretion, warmth. Survival was the only issue every minute of the day, every day of the month, every month of the year. There was no sweet memory of the past, no swelling of optimism for the future; there was only the stinking, suffering, horrific present.

The German SS managed to strip away all sense of self from most of the millions of prisoners by subjecting them to the cruelest of atrocities, by destroying any hope for a future. But there were those who insisted, quietly, on making it through. There were those who would not let the boundary, however thin, between themselves and their environment dissolve. They resisted, they said no, they retained their dignity. These survivors are fascinating to everyone; but for me their tales stir an especially fervent interest. Certainly I never thought that I would have to go without food for months at a time or sleep in a bed of urine and feces or withstand all the monstrous pressures of the Nazi camps in order to appreciate life's most precious gifts. Yet I was always attracted to the test of the spirit, and I always knew that it would have to be an extreme situation, indeed, that would draw that strength of spirit to the surface.

One of my favorite stories was David Howarth's *We Die Alone* ("*On mourra seul,*" Pascal), which was about a young

Norwegian man, Jan Baalsrud, who attempted to sabotage
the Germans as they occupied his country during the early
years of World War II. He barely escaped capture, swimming through freezing channels, skiing and walking for
miles and miles without warm clothing, trying to reach the
neutral border of Sweden. Crushed by an avalanche, he lay
unconscious in the snow for several days until severe frostbite turned to gangrene. When he awoke, he could no
longer walk. On a plateau with blizzards whipping up from
every direction, he spent twenty-seven days and nights without food. He was buried alive under four feet of snow for a
week, and for the rest of his twenty-seven-day ordeal he had
only a sip of brandy every two days.

In an anti-German effort, men from the towns who had
discovered him came up every few nights to keep him alive.
Several more weeks passed. Knowing that the gangrene was
spreading to his legs, Jan cut off his own toes with a blunt
pocket knife. Finally, taking great risk of being caught by
the Germans, the townsfolk brought him to a cove to regain
warmth and strength, and a Lapp offered to carry him on
his sled to the Swedish border. His weight was then seventy-
eight pounds, half of what it was when he debarked on his
mission. But he made it. It took three months in a Swedish
hospital to save his feet, but he made it.

There are countless cases of people exhausted from hunger and exposure who give up; the strength of will fades
simultaneously with the strength of body. That is why Jan
Baalsrud's story excites me so. The physical breakdown was
complete, there was no reserve from which to draw, and Jan
himself says that the temptation to capitulate, to close his
eyes and die peacefully, grew stronger and stronger each day.
Yet the spirit within that lifeless body was indomitable and

could seemingly take any and every abuse. At one point during the twenty-seven-day nightmare on the plateau Jan recalls thinking that he would most likely lose his feet and perhaps his legs, but that he would grow tremendously in experience.

Of course, Jan Baalsrud and the few who managed to live through Auschwitz and the other death camps comprise a category of survivors unique unto themselves in that it was war. Their situation was directly created by a merciless enemy, and their decision to remain alive must in part have been ignited by anger and the wish to one day retaliate, if only by their power to bear witness.

But there are other life and death experiences that present the same problems, although the ultimate escape is from Nature herself rather than from a calculating human force. The most recent case is probably that of the Uruguayan soccer team whose plane crashed in the Andes and especially of the two boys who, having played each last desperate card, dug deep past their physical potential to the life force that enabled them to climb an impossible mountain to rescue themselves and their friends. When there were no more calories to burn, when strength had faded to nothing months before, when frostbite was so severe that walking a few steps took a monumental effort, the boys pressed on. The need for dignity and the will to resist giving up are subtle, almost mysterious threads that somehow allow a person to transcend what once were the outer limits.

And in the sports world, the marathon swimmer also faces this extreme moment over and over again when actual physical strength and conscious presence of mind have long since been drained. The battle for survival is against an indefatigable foe, the sea. When you lose as much as ten to fifteen pounds in just a few hours (I once lost twenty-four pounds in forty hours in the North Sea), and when you have been shaking with the ice-cold of 55-degree water for perhaps an entire day without relief, and when you have been seasick from swallowing the sea water for a number of hours, there is simply nothing left. This is the point beyond which muscular coordination, a beautiful stroke and god-given talent no longer mean anything. Neither genetic predisposition toward great endurance nor the background of months and years of dedicated training count in the least. Now the words of encouragement from the coach's boat are absolutely empty. And since there is simply nothing left, you have to dig deeper and deeper into your gut until you arrive at that same core of pride and dignity that the survivors know. Every minute seems like an hour, every hour is filled with constant discomfort and moments of excruciating pain. You lose sight of the original goal, and all the pain seems purposeless. You want to quit so many times, but there is a quiet burning near the heart that makes you clench your teeth and refuse to go out a quitter. You roll over on your back, you throw off your goggles, you say no, you sigh, you cry, and that quiet burning somehow makes you roll back over and pick the left arm up again. The body is 100 percent spent, but the will still blazes brightly.

I read the polar expedition stories over and over again when I was a kid. And I always fantasize about them during the gruesome lows of a swim. The best two stories were those of Robert F. Scott and Sir Ernest Henry Shackleton —both compellingly written, with the English gift of understatement. Scott made his last attempt to reach the South Pole in 1910–1913. He and four men reached the Pole one month after the Norwegian explorer Roald Amundsen.

Disappointed but proud, they began their return journey. One man died of frostbite and another died when going out into a blizzard to get help for his three remaining comrades. Scott and the other two died only thirteen miles from fuel, warmth and food because a blizzard raged for an unexpected seven days. They had fuel and food enough for two days. They couldn't make it through that final death blow, but the hardships they overcame to reach that point were seemingly beyond human capacity. As testimony to their undying spirit, Scott wrote to a friend a few days before their death:

We are in a desperate state, feet frozen, etc. No fuel and a long way from food. We did intend to finish ourselves when things proved like this . . . but it would do your heart good to be in our tent, to hear our songs and the cheery conversation as to what we will do when we get to Hut Point.

    —Cherry-Garrard, *The Worst Journey in the World,* p. 528

The glow of the life force carried Scott and his comrades long after muscular power and ingenuity had failed. And perhaps the most interesting notes from their diaries are those which indicate that, even in the midst of freezing and starving to death, they actually seemed to revel in the extremity of their predicament. The very day of his death, Scott wrote again to a friend: "What lots and lots I could tell you of this journey. How much better has it been than lounging in too great comfort at home."

It isn't that every painful experience offers ultimate awareness of life's intrinsic values. It's that the most extreme conditions require the most extreme response, and for some individuals, the call to that response is vitality itself. Even knowing that he was to die within a very few hours, Scott deemed the severity of his journey worthwhile. Jan Baalsrud felt that his experience was worth the possible loss of his feet. I am quite sure that none of the concentration camp survivors would say that his hell was worth anything at all; however, if abstractions are possible in their case, many of them have said that the strength of will they were forced to tap has since been a source of enlightenment throughout their lives.

I would not feign to compare my swimming conditions, however difficult they might be compared to any other sport or even any other everyday endeavor, with those of people who are truly down to life or death without compromise. My point is that, if the circumstances are extreme enough, will is the only thing that can pull you through. And if you have shown the strength of will to pull through, you seem to consider yourself much the better for it. I think that Shackleton's story is always the most inspiring for me—and probably the story that most closely touches upon the difficulties of a marathon swim.

Ernest Shackleton and a crew of twenty-seven men set sail from England on the ship *Endurance* to become the first group to cross the continent of Antarctica on foot. Still 1,200 miles from the continent and 1,500 miles from the nearest inhabited islands to the north, their ship was caught and squeezed by thousands of square miles of ice floes and bergs. They were wedged at that point for over a year, hoping that the ice would eventually break up and give them a passage to open sea. But the ice finally crushed the *Endurance* and drew her under, so that the twenty-eight men were out on the unstable ice without a chance of being rescued or making land themselves. It was the year 1915, so radio communications weren't sophisticated enough to be of service. They had dogs and sleds, three lifeboats, and limited supplies. They killed seals and penguins in the summer and nearly starved in the winter when the sun never shone and the animals migrated north. Severe frostbite was constant. The ice kept breaking up, and they had to save themselves hurriedly by transporting everything to the next stable block.

Six months later they ran out of fuel, so Shackleton and four men set sail in a suicidal venture to reach a tiny island more than 800 miles away where supplies had been left by a former expedition. The lifeboat was twenty-one feet long and six feet, three inches across the beam. They lived through this impossible journey and at last made it to a whaling town, providing rescue for the remaining men down on the ice who had been fighting for their lives for over two years. All twenty-eight men survived.

Shackleton observed something about his heroic struggle in the lifeboat that strikes a most sensitive chord within the heart of the proven marathon swimmer:

Unlike the land where courage and the simple will to endure can often see a man through, the struggle against the sea is an act of physical combat and there is no escape. It is a battle against a tireless enemy in which man never actually wins; the most that he can hope for is not to be defeated.

—Lansing, *Endurance*, pp. 213–214

This is the same battle in which we swimmers engage. Not only is an extraordinary will required to overcome the hellish circumstances; but will to the nth degree must be summoned to press on in the relentless effort against Her Majesty the sea.

I identify strongly with Shackleton's victory. In survival against the elements, one exerts more of an effort than in any other life situation. And in marathon swimming, one exerts more of an effort than for any other sport. All survivors tell of the depressing death of time. Marathon swimmers must also cope with the death of time. After all, the structure of time is probably one of civilization's most comforting creations. Defining the day, the year, one's life, in terms of time lends some sense of purpose. The measure of time assures the worth of the past and growth of the future. But in fighting for one's survival, the death of time is disconcerting in that one moment can't in any way be distinguished from another; the purposive nature of time is destroyed because there is no concept that the end is actually a possibility. There is no faith that any action might prove useful for the future.

Imagine swimming continually for fifteen hours. Fifteen hours in rough, cold ocean water. Fifteen hours of unconsciously doing the same stroke that you have been doing since you were ten years old. You can't hear because of the caps, and you can't see because of the dark, fogged goggles. You can't think because the human mind is not geared to focus for any lengthy period of time, so your thoughts drift in delirium and soon time is more distorted than ever. As far as you know, you are in the middle of nowhere and any effort you might produce to stroke again won't necessarily bring you any closer to your goal because much of the time you can't seem to remember what the goal is. It is clear that your ordeal is without end, and there is only one thing you somehow sense—that the choice to abandon the struggle and climb aboard the ship would be to fragment your pride beyond repair. Survival is keeping one's dignity intact.

Like the survivor's situation, the swimmer's extremity forces him to abandon civilized concerns; satisfaction comes from the simple things—food, excretion, rhythm, sensations. There is nothing else. The options for focus are very few at that point, and the additional factor of exhaustion brings one down to the basics. I will go for hours trying to urinate. I am so thoroughly preoccupied with it that I can hear it sloshing back and forth in the bladder; it requires a profound concentration, sometimes for as many as five or six hours, to force the urine to pass. Food is another basic item of intense interest for a swimmer in the throes of exhaustion. Shackleton's men told of anticipating a swallow of condensed milk for a week, waking with screams in the middle of the night with the fear that they had missed their ration. My food every hour on the hour is about 3,000 calories worth of pure glucose. And occasionally I am given a digestive biscuit to help absorb some of the sea water in the stomach. I have been so intent on receiving that cookie and thinking only of its taste, color and texture for hours on end that I have screamed for it in a voice filled with immediate desperation when a quiet word during a breath would suffice to get my trainer to offer one over the side.

And the focus on counting, on playing games with numbers of strokes to provide the sanity of at least short-term goals, always has a hypnotizing effect. The rhythm of a hand entering the water each and every second so that the count will average sixty per minute is so balanced, so monotonous, that at times you feel as though the sound of your hand slapping the surface is the only sound on earth. All the men in both Scott's and Shackleton's parties, limited by their extreme environment, told at some point of focusing on the sound of their boots crunching the ice until something akin to a deep hypnotic trance took place. Food, excretion and sensations are the basics during extremity.

Another common bond between survivors of extremity is that you grow more attached to people in a very short time. Certainly any group of people who work together and respect each other lay the foundation for lifelong friendships. But I have noticed that in marathon swimming the respect is fanatical. I have swum tremendously difficult races against Egyptian competitors, for example, with whom I share nothing in common as far as everyday life is concerned and with whom I can't even communicate because of the language barrier. But when we are lying in hospital beds next to each other after a particularly grueling marathon, there is such an emotional pitch among us that pride and mutual respect and deep understanding seal an intense comradeship.

The associations, if only from an emotional point of view, between survival situations and marathon swims are numerous. But the common denominator is dignity, grace under pressure. Under the murderous pressures of extremity, there is a need to sustain the power and the wholeness of self when all else has been stripped away. One of the first rewards after a marathon swim is to cross over the same course by plane or boat. Ironically, as you sit in the seat of a plane that can cross Lake Ontario in twenty minutes, you swell with glorious emotional pride to gaze down at the whitecaps you battled for three-fourths of a day. The integrity and self-esteem gained from winning the battle against extremity are the richest treasures in my life. When asked why, I say that marathon swimming is the most difficult physical, intellectual and emotional battleground I have encountered, and each time I win, each time I touch the other shore, I feel worthy of any other challenge life has to offer.

9. The Cuba Swim

~~~~~~

THE LIFE SPAN of an athletic career is not always determined by age or physical competence. At twenty-eight, I have no doubt that I will be as strong, as fast, as fit and as physically competent ten years from now as I am today. But I have other interests, other dreams. In my typically all-or-nothing fashion, I have given 110 percent of myself to a sport for almost twenty years. And the sport, worthy as it is, has repaid me with personal treasures. Each extreme moment demanded that I dissect the mind more carefully and with each new dissection I grew. But now I sense that there is very little growth potential left for me in marathon swimming. The end approaches, but it is not a tragic one; it is filled with life. There will be one last swim. One last supreme effort. I am preparing to reach further than I have ever grasped and the prospect thrills me as if I were fifteen again and dreaming of Olympic medals.

My strongest recurring fantasy goes something like this: A devil appears during my sleep and in the darkness offers me unlimited physical prowess. I can run the mile in one minute, pole-vault 600 feet, and so forth. In return, I must suggest the name of a person I know who will be killed. When one is dealing with the devil, deception is not possible. The person I choose to die must be very close to me. The fantasy continues as I then use my physical prowess to more realistic ends than one-minute miles: Olympic golds in every sport, Wimbledon titles, repetitive breaking of world records year after year.

I suppose the base interpretation of my Faustian fantasy is that I want to do something unprecedented in the world of sports—something so outrageously difficult it would go unmatched for many, many years. I want to bid my love affair with marathon swimming a spectacular farewell. I want to accomplish the unimaginable.

In April 1977, I spread all the nautical charts of the world across my living-room rug. I spent three weeks making lists, checking mileage and water temperatures, eliminating some projects, reassessing others. I finally came up with the ideal swim. A swim in the Hellenic concept of sport—impossible yet somehow possible. Come July 1978, I am going to start off on the longest open-water swim in history. The greatest endurance feat in history. I will swim nonstop from Cuba to Florida. Nonstop from Havana to Marathon Key. One hundred thirty miles in the open ocean; sixty hours of continuous swimming.

THE MANHATTAN ISLAND SWIM left me knocking at many doors that had once been beyond my reach. I was doing exactly what I had always done, but it seemed that I had moved from an empty sand lot to Madison Square Garden. It may have been the Garden with less than full capacity, but it was nevertheless the Garden. The irony was that I had learned this commercial approach so late in my career. My friend and trainer Buck Dawson thought of writing a book to extol the great athletes who missed the Olympic games because of war, illness or injury. There were many. But even more great athletes have been denied recognition by the public because of the warped image created by the media and the big money of American sports.

From 1970 through 1975 I had traveled around the world six times, completing long-distance swims of tremendous difficulty. I had swum twenty hours in Lake Ontario, twenty-four hours in the rough Australian surf, forty hours in the frozen North Sea, and a couple of dozen other feats I would think long and hard about before attempting again. But no one outside my peer group and the loyal *Sports Illustrated* fans had ever heard of me. It didn't seem important at the time, but age and experience and disrespect on the circuit provoked a change of heart. I cultivated a desire for recognition outside my athletic peer group. The Manhattan Island swim took less than eight hours; it was not easy because no marathons are easy, but it was one of the less painful swims I had done. It was the only marathon after which I needed no medical attention or hospitalization, but ironically, it was the one that put me on the map. When I thought it over, it wasn't so ironic after all.

The three sports in which it probably takes the most time to reach national or world-caliber level (both short-term, day-to-day time and long-term, year-after-year time) are swimming, rowing and cycling. They are the heavy conditioning sports that require hours of LSD (long slow distance), weight work for strength, and hours of intervals and sprints. Even long-distance running is not so time-consuming because the type of necessary training presents little variation. I have trained for the 26-mile, 365-yard marathon by running twelve miles a day at a six-minute pace, in addition to two days of interval sprints, such as a set of twenty 440-yard runs on the watch, and then one long run of fifteen to twenty-two miles. I am not a world-class runner; I have never tried to be. And yet I contend that I could and will go the marathon under 2 hours, 40 minutes. I have already broken the respectable three-hour mark for the regulation distance, and I can safely say that there was no day during that short training period (three months) when I was thoroughly incapacitated. However, when I train for a marathon swim of over thirty miles, I put in workouts three times a day of two hours each, as well as the weight workouts and the long swims of ten and twelve hours (hours, not miles) on the weekends. When I am running seriously, I can still play squash, write, speak at functions, travel, practice the clarinet and socialize. When I am swimming seriously, I can't do anything whatsoever but swim.

I always thought it most unfair that the athletes who worked the hardest were the least recognized and the poorest paid, if paid at all. I didn't question whether great baseball players were finer athletes than great rowers; I just knew that baseball players never practiced the eight hours a day demanded by the conditioning sports, and I thought that guts and hard work should be on the other side of the recognition/money equation. By 1975 my eyes had finally been opened to the ways of the world, and at twenty-five, figuring that I had put in fifteen very gutsy years, I set out to pursue the commercial route of the rare Weismullers, Crabbes, de Varonas, and Spitzes by turning my swimming talent and hard work into cold cash. The catch was that I refused to compromise my athletic integrity. An event still had to inspire me with its own merit.

The other side of the recognition/money equation, it seems, is media exposure. Tennis is *numero uno* in the public eye, and the tennis players are paid like *numero unos.* Rowers slave away for years in unknown rivers and remain unknown themselves. So, as a good friend aptly expressed it when I left the pro circuit in disgust in 1975, "If you're going to continue to pursue these masochistic monsters, why don't you at least do them where everyone will know about them?" Hence the Manhattan Island swim. Both the first unsuccessful attempt and the later success were huge media draws in New York, and as the saying goes, if you're known in New York, you're known everywhere. The *New York Times* put me on page one both times, with photos. This was news, not sports. Every television and radio station in the city gave my swim top priority for the day's news. The *New York Daily News* filled their centerfold with pictures of the World Trade Center buildings and the Statue of Liberty with a tiny speck of an arm reaching out of the spray in between. And the aftermath, in terms of the media, was an onslaught of national interest. *People, Sports Illustrated, Glamour, Esquire, Mademoiselle,* the *Village Voice, Vogue, Seventeen*—all did feature stories on me. On television, I was in a half-hour documentary with Jim Bouton, I rode a killer whale on Howard Cosell's show, *Saturday Night Live* featured me in their film segment, Newsweek Broadcasting did a documentary, I did the *Today* show and the rest of the talk-show circuit, and I had the dubious distinction of appearing on *To Tell the Truth.*

Such flares of minor stardom are not impressive in themselves. First of all, it is superficial exaggeration, mostly fiction at that, that perpetrates the myth of the "star"; you must take it all with a grain of salt. And second, what impressed me was not the national attention; it was that the whole payoff thudded on my doorstep as a result of the third-least difficult swim of my career. And along with the media interest came occasional chances to pad my formerly nonexistent bank account. I didn't leap into an enviable tax bracket, but I was suddenly paying the rent with change and grinning with the satisfaction of having made a nonmedia sport pay me back for everything I had invested. I was speaking for $1,000 a throw at corporate motivational meetings, Saxton paid me to do their English Channel documentary, I was writing for several national magazines, I had my own column with one of the women's magazines, I was offered announcing jobs with two of the networks, and I signed a three-year endorsement contract with a swimming goggles and squash rackets manufacturer.

I WAS AT HOME one night about a month after the Manhattan Island swim when the phone rang. It was a friend from ABC who wanted to introduce me to an admirer. I wasn't interested. She said it was Woody Allen. I changed my mind. Said I would be home for half an hour. The phone rang five minutes later.

"Hello."

"Hello. Diana?"

"Yes."

"This is Woody. Woody Allen. I hope I'm not disturbing you."

"Not at all. How are things in the movie business?"

"Oh, pretty good. Listen, you're probably busy, getting in some extra push-ups or something. Maybe I should call some other time."

"I understand you're a basketball fan. Play yourself?"

"Oh, not really—I mean, nothing to speak of, a little one-on-one. You know, that was really incredible, what you did. I'd like to talk to you some time."

"How about tomorrow?"

"Tomorrow? Great."

Woody turned out to be one of the treasures one stumbles upon perhaps once a decade. He became a friend whom I would see two or three times a year, and I cherish those exchanges, however infrequent. His integrity inspires me. I have always been extremely disciplined, with an occasional touch of expectedly extreme spontaneity, and I learned at a tender age that life is too short to fill with unobsessed time. But Woody makes even my style appear indecisive. He is intently devoted to the creation of his films, the writing, directing, acting, and so forth. When a film is in production, Woody is incommunicado. He is also devoted to the clarinet, the Knicks, and a few select friends. My own focus has narrowed to a pinpoint through knowing Woody. The most amusing encounter was probably the night of his surprise birthday party.

It was the dead of winter. I was in the midst of a sweaty, intensely competitive game of squash at the Fifth Avenue Racquet Club when a knock sounded at the little court door. There was a telephone call for me. I was annoyed and rude. "Take a message and tell them I'll call back." Slam!

The call was from a friend who had evidently been trying without success to reach me for weeks. There was to be a surprise birthday party for Woody that night at Michael's Pub, the East Side joint where he plays clarinet with a swing band every Monday. She said I should arrive at eight on the button. Five minutes early or late and he would see me and guess something was up. But I don't have a present. No one gives presents. But I've only got jeans. That was fine; she said "the place is a dive."

At which time it was seven-forty. I dashed up to the locker room to find that someone had mistakenly clamped his padlock on my locker. I had been playing at the club for over a year and had never had problems with stealing, locks, or anything else. I flitted from court to court, tapping on the doors with my racket. "Excuse me, could you possibly have put your lock on the wrong locker by mistake?" Five minutes of that to no avail and I realized that it was go as is or no go at all. I borrowed five dollars from the cashier and bounded out onto Fifth Avenue in search of a taxi. The wind was howling. The temperature was 19 degrees. I was wearing a pair of Adidas track shorts, a mesh-thin T-shirt, a soaked headband, unmatched socks and sneakers. No coat.

I arrived precisely at eight, and for those of you who have never frequented Michael's Pub, I can vouch for one very distinct observation which I made that first night. The place is no dive. As I bounced over the threshold with athletic grace, the maitre d', in full dress tuxedo, stared in disbelief. I had the upper hand, however, as I caught him off his guard, and when I announced that I was in Woody's party, he offered an elegant arm and escorted me to a chair at the front. As you can imagine, all heads turned—and stayed with me most of the evening. I decided not to apologize, and my confidence let it be understood that athletes had some sort of dress license which was not to be questioned. Berry Berenson in her one-shouldered gown and her husband Tony Perkins in his immaculate tux could have cared less. Paul Simon never even noticed. And Diana Vreeland, the former long-time editor of *Vogue,* kept asking me with absolute sincerity where I bought my simply divine little shorts. (I later appeared on the front page of the *New York Post* with Jackie Kennedy Onassis—Jackie in a lovely summer print and me in a handsome Lacoste shirt. If Woody set the precedent of combining sneakers with tuxedo, I suppose I was the first to get away with sneakers and a dress.)

Not all of the opportunities which arose because of the Manhattan swim were as much fun, however, as making friends with Woody. Some of the possibilities seemed enticing at the time and later proved to be boring, embarrassing, or simply a waste of time and energy. Vaseline Intensive Care hired me to tour the country in behalf of their product. It was a good product and the company itself treated me exceptionally well, but I found the demands of talk-show advertising demeaning and swore that I would have to be in desperate financial straits indeed to ever accept a product endorsement tour again. Commercials are straightforward. Everyone knows that you are being paid to say whatever you say, and the sponsor derives a benefit anyway. But on this endorsement tour I was supposed to appear for television, radio and newspaper interviews in the top ten media cities in the United States, excluding New York. The subject of the interview would be me, my fascinating past history—swimming, sharks, delirium, grease and so forth—and somehow, smoothly self-introduced within the interview time, I was expected to spend at least sixty seconds talking about the product. And worse, legality dictated that I had to present the full, registered title of the product—Extra Strength Vaseline Intensive Care Lotion for Problem Hands—a mouthful which defies smooth spontaneity. The ultimate mortification would come when I had to dip under my seat and pronounce, "I just happen to have a bottle with me."

Other offers seemed uninteresting and proved to be most worthwhile. ABC invited me to participate in the Superstars, and my initial reaction was to decline because I found all those contrived television events so moronic; I couldn't picture myself bounding over the hurdles with a silly television grin on my face and fishing for witticisms in answer to the usual irrelevant questions ("What does your boyfriend think of your athletic prowess?"). But my second guess about the Superstars was that it would be a golden opportunity to meet twenty-three of the best women athletes alive. And that it was. Althea Gibson, at forty-eight, was still in amazing control of her tennis game. I loved her answer to one of the interview questions: "Althea, being black must have been a very powerful incentive to prove yourself within the stuffy white tennis establishments of those days. Would you say that being black was the biggest factor in driving you toward greatness?" Althea: "Why no, Keith, I would say it was simply god-given ability."

Martina Navratilova was strong like a bull. Wyomia Tyus was grace personified. But aside from the handful of well-knowns, most of us relative unknowns shared a magnetic bond. We were the very best at what we did in an era when women's sports were just beginning to be accepted, we had all been unfeted, unheralded and grossly unpaid compared to our male counterparts, and we were fiercely proud. There were the best softball player in the country, the best basketball player, the best volleyball player, the best golfer, the best boxer, the best pool player, the best speed skater, the best skier, the best diver, the best football player. And I loved them all.

One of the memorable scenes of the Superstars that year involved Monique Proulx, Formula I driver from France.

Monique was a refreshing change of pace from us jocks; if there was any stereotype, it was sort of boyish—most of us were short-haired, wide-shouldered, thin-hipped, gum-chewing jocks. Monique wore six-inch platform shoes, blue jeans so tight that she could never take a stride of more than a foot, and a skintight jersey with silver sequins flashing across her chest, spelling out "You have to have balls to drive the Formula I." She would drive into the parking lot in a cloud of dust in her custom-made Porsche, and I think she threw the softball an unprecedented distance of fifteen feet. I liked her. We all had to give either Billie Jean or Keith Jackson a sixty-second interview that they could later pull out during the event. Question posed to Monique: "Well, Monique, we all know that you are a very competent driver, but how are you going to do here in the Superstars? I mean, you are very thin. How are you going to do in these tough events like rowing and cycling and the 440 against these powerful women?" Monique's response: "Well, fuck you, buddy, 'cause I drives zat car two hundred forty fucking miles an hour and zere izn't anybody here who can drive zat car as fucking fast as I do." Hear! Hear!

IF THE MANHATTAN ISLAND swim left me knocking at many doors, the Cuba swim is going to swing those doors wide open; in fact, it's going to blow them right off their hinges! Marathon Key lies 130 statute miles (113 nautical miles) from Havana. This will be a legitimate marathon, nonstop without touching boat, people or cage (except accidental brushing with a leg or shoulder), and with no external aids, such as flippers, wet suits, flotation devices or drugs. "Open water" means that there is no free ride from river currents and that there is no protection from wind or waves or shoreline. There are cases of men in Argentina who have been in the water for eighty and more hours, but that was a question of staying awake for as long as possible until the speed of the current takes you to your destination. There are many swims across large bodies of water where the swimmer swims a few hours and then climbs on board to rest a few hours, but these are never recorded as marathon swims; they always sound extremely impressive in terms of mileage and hours spent in the water, but they are not accepted as official records of any sort in the serious long-distance swimming world. Open-water swims are the most difficult and the most respected of marathons. Every foot of progress must be made by the swimmer's own strength. To date, the longest open-water swim was across Lake Michigan from Chicago to Benton Harbor, a distance of 60 miles. The distance record is held by two men; the first one came in during a race in 1963, setting the record for speed over the 60 miles. Abo-Heif of Egypt touched the Michigan shore in 34 hours, 38 minutes, and Ted Erikson of Chicago finished in 37 hours, 31 minutes in the same race.

To compare the Cuba swim with other marathon swimming feats, one should look at a few of the mileage and approximate hours-spent-in-water figures for the swims that are by far the most revered throughout the world. The English Channel is 21 miles across, and the record is now under 9 hours. Double crossings of the Channel are open-water swims as far as I'm concerned (although they are technically not listed as such because the swimmer is allowed ten minutes on the other shore); in any case, a double crossing of the Channel is 42 miles (actually more because you are swept side to side by the tide), and the record is just under 20 hours. Lake Ontario is 32 miles across from

Toronto to Niagara Falls, and the record there is some 15 hours. The Catalina Island swim (to the mainland of California) is 22 miles, and the record is about 8 hours. The Bay of Naples (Capri to Naples) is also 22 miles, and the record is also about 8 hours. Lac St. Jean, Quebec, is 25 miles across, and the record is 8 hours. The Strait of Juan de Fuca between the State of Washington and Canada is only 11 miles across, but has taken 11 hours to cross because the water temperature is in the forties. The Farallon Islands lie 21 miles from San Francisco and have taken 13 1/2 hours to conquer. And probably the most difficult open-water swim to date, although not the longest, has been the crossing of the North Channel of the Irish Sea, 22 miles in 47-degree water; the record is around 21 hours.

There are other respectable open-water swims but none of them, including the current nonstop distance record of 60 miles, can compare with a swim from Cuba to Florida. When we speak of swimming continuously for over 60 hours in open sea water to cover 130 miles, we are speaking of a world record that will stand for many decades.

Aside from the phenomenal distance, the Cuba swim poses several other problems. The first is the Gulf Stream. If you are swimming across Lake Ontario or Lake Michigan— or even the English Channel, where the tides are relatively uniform and expected—you simply plod ahead at whatever pace you can handle. If you are swimming from Miami to the Bahamas, you can find the axis of the Gulf Stream and add the speed of the current to your swimming speed. But in a swim from Havana to Marathon Key, the Gulf Stream is more of a problem than a benefit. Marathon Key is not 0 degrees due north of Havana, but the essential swimming direction is north, so you must cross this powerful body of current in heading toward your goal; depending on the wind direction and speed, you may even have to swim directly west against the Gulf Stream to compensate for being dragged too far to the east. The average flow of the current is three knots per hour, faster than the average swimming speed, especially over such a long period. In its axis, the current speed is over five knots. In addition to its power, the Gulf Stream has uncertainty on its side. It is a belt of approximately 25 miles in width; some days the belt lies just outside the Cuban border, which would be the most fortunate case for a swimmer—you could use your initial strength to battle the Stream and then head straight for Marathon Key with at least one big worry out of the way. But other days, it seems, the belt lies way up parallel to the Florida Keys. And on still other days, the belt undulates between the Keys and Cuba, so that you don't necessarily approach it directly from the south nor do you necessarily swim through it directly toward west. The absolute clincher comes when you take a look at the daily Gulf Stream pattern charts for any given year. There is no pattern. It is virtually impossible to predict the latitude coordinates of the Gulf Stream between the Keys and Cuba on a day-to-day basis—an impossibility which could be of dire importance to a swimmer.

The next problem with this swim is turbulence. Except for a quarter mile at either side, there is obviously no land protection; the Gulf Stream with its speed causes rough seas, and the unconfined wind in combination doesn't produce a glassy surface. Swimming is much more of an effort in waves than on a flat surface; sometimes if I go out to do a six-hour training swim and discover that the sea is exceptionally rough, I put in four hours and reap the rewards of a harder workout than six in calm water. Also, rough water—especially rough salt water—invariably means hours of unpleasant seasickness. High seas in a fresh-water lake can cause nausea and vomiting because of the tossing and bobbing and rolling. But rough salt water is infinitely worse because there is the added misery of swallowing. Every swimmer accidentally takes in a certain amount of water over a period of hours. The waves are not predictable, and as you become more tired and lose the physical strength to breathe high or the mental clarity to concentrate continually on avoiding swallowing, you take in gulp after gulp. Gulps of fresh water are all right, but salt water is deadly. Imagine finishing up a feeding of 3,000 calories of pure liquid glucose which you have had to force-feed because it was so voluminous and so nauseatingly sweet; then imagine settling into your stroke again and being hit flat in the face by a three-footer. Within one second a mouthful of salt water joins the rich glucose in your stomach; very few mouthfuls go by before you begin retching your guts up.

And the last major stickler of the Cuba swim is the question of sharks. As far as I'm concerned, there is no question at all. The Florida Strait is an area where sharks are prevalent; many fins are sighted every day of the year by fishermen, servicemen, pleasure craft and even aircraft. With *Jaws* and the current media hype over sharks, I am frequently asked if there is really any scientifically based reason to fear shark attacks while swimming a long distance; my answer is that sharks were a little-understood source of danger with a significant history of human attacks long before they were a media hype and I'm not willing to be the guinea pig in retesting the already-disproven theory that, if left alone, sharks will leave you alone. A few years ago when I went to swim off the Great Barrier Reef in Australia I was told upon arrival that I would have to swim in a cage that would be towed behind a power craft. I was unbearably cocky in those days and said that I had no intention of swimming in a cage, thanks just the same. The next day I was on a short training swim, not far from shore, and I spotted fins at every glance. I decided I might try the cage after all. It was constructed out of wire road mesh in the shape of a room twenty feet long by fifteen feet wide by ten feet deep, and was supported by styrofoam flotation devices at the corners. I suppose I was grateful for the cage because that particular swim couldn't have been done without it; sharks bumped the sides and the front continually. Their sight is so poor that they probably brush by the splashing swimmer to smell it and to touch it with their skin perceptors. But on the other hand . . . The cage was necessary, but it was also ridiculous. It was so confining that I had to stop every ten or twenty strokes, especially after I became tired and disoriented, to position myself back in the middle. I completed the swim in 24 hours, 13 minutes; without the cage—that is, without the sharks—I would have finished closer to 18 hours. Also, I broke three fingers of my right hand at the eleventh hour when I came up unawares on the front of the cage and took a full hard stroke into the road mesh instead of air. The broken fingers made the remaining hours of the swim extremely uncomfortable.

There are ocean swims where sharks are spotted occasionally but where there is not a serious problem and a cage is not needed, such as in the Caribbean or off the west coast of Mexico. But the area between Cuba and the Florida Keys is a proven danger zone. Repellents have not been workably developed as of the moment. A couple of marksmen on board with rifles is not out of the question for a short time, but for sixty hours, with two full periods of darkness, rifles are ineffectual. A cage is the only answer, but I can't afford to have any unnecessary hours of swimming tacked on this time, so the cage must be a sophisticated one.

In the summer of 1977 I went to a friend who has sailed competitively at the highest levels of international racing. His name is Rich de Moulin, and besides knowledgeable advice concerning currents and course, he suggested a design for a shark cage. There will be two aluminum pontoons, each forty feet in length and three feet in diameter. These pontoons will be floated on the surface, parallel to each other, twenty feet apart. Aluminum caging will be built under the pontoons in the shape of a room without a roof so that the floor of the room will be twelve feet under the surface and all four sides of the room will extend to about three feet above the surface. The back wall of the room will operate like a drawbridge so that I can duck in and out of the cage without actually grabbing it for support to climb over the top. The pontoons and the tops of the front and back wall will be rubberized so that if I inadvertently brush by one side with a leg or shoulder or hand it won't be a problem. The pontoons will be filled with gasoline, which is less dense than water, and a small outboard motor will be at the end of each pontoon so that almost unlimited gas will feed into the fuel lines of the motors. A walkable bridge will be built up across the back end of the cage, sturdy enough to support four or five men, from which a driver can manipulate the cage by a steering device rigged by cable to the two motors. I will be swimming in the middle of the cage, breathing to the left, where the small navigational boat will be cruising just outside the left pontoon. The driver of the cage will be communicating with my trainer and following me.

Jellyfish can also become a real problem. They often float

in giant schools on the surface, and if the trainer doesn't see the tentacles in time, you swim into the gelatinous mass. You are at the mercy of the barblike stinging until you can find clear water. Some swimmers become nauseated after a few severe stings—perhaps an allergic reaction. I'm not affected that way, but that stinging can be quite painful for a time. Another minor animal problem is gulls. They think you are a splashing fish, and they swoop down to peck at your white bathing cap. It only takes a whisk of your hand to get rid of them, but they can frighten the hell out of you if you are unsuspecting. Other animals can be annoying in other bodies of water. (In Lake Ontario the leeches attach themselves to your skin, and you have to make a concentrated effort to pry them off.) But in the Cuba swim it's primarily a question of sharks.

Rich took his cage design to a friend who is the best aluminum boat builder in the world in the fall of 1977 so that a finished product would be tested and ready for use by May. Rich has also helped me plot the course. After swimmers, sailors are the subjects most sensitive to wind, tide, current and the whims of the sea. His first discovery was that a swim from the Keys to Cuba was out of the question and that it would have to be the other way around. He plotted my swimming speed as it degenerates over the hours, along with the different possible Gulf Stream configurations, and the different possible wind directions and velocities—the result was an approximate sixty hours, which assumed neither ideal nor disastrous conditions but something in between. He spent a month making a detailed expense budget of crew and equipment needed. The shark cage is the big expense because it has to be custom-built. With the cage, the operational budget is approximately $85,000.

Most of the swims I have done, even the very difficult and the tricky ones, have been fly-by-night operations. In the past, if I have needed a boat or two, I have gone down to the docks in a strange town to ask strangers to join me on my adventure. Or I have gone on the local radio shows saying I needed two English-speaking people to help me across the Bay of Naples. No pay. And at the time I did all those difficult and tricky swims, that was exactly the way I wanted it. My highest expectation was in reaching the other shore, and nothing else interested me. The Cuba swim is of a different era. Recognition and money and future attract me now. But I am relieved to discover, as I begin the most serious stage of training, that my highest expectation has remained the same. When I fall asleep at night, I don't conjure up images of great sums of money and my name in lights; I have a sensual fantasy of struggling through that fifty-ninth hour, of passing finally through the agony to the ecstasy, of touching the sand at Marathon Key. This fantasy is what attracts me first and foremost and what inspires me to train so devotedly, as it always has. My motives are more complex than they have ever been, but the nature of the drive is still single-minded. It is now March 1978, and I am focused on only one thing—crossing those 130 miles, lasting those sixty hours, reaching that Florida coast. This is the big one that is so outrageous and so nearly impossible that I would be one of only a handful who would even attempt it, much less make it. This is the big one that marks the end of a grand era for me.

I began training, in effect, on July 1, 1977, precisely one year before the swim. The first six months were spent doing what I call building a gentle reserve. I was in fairly good shape before July, so the step-up was not too severe. For the

month of July I ran ten miles every morning in seventy
minutes or under (by the last four days I was coming in at
sixty-three minutes). I did two heavy Nautilus workouts per
week. I skipped rope for a half-hour each day, and I played
squash for an average of four hours. (The squash part of this
program has nothing to do with Cuba or conditioning for
swimming. I simply want to be good at the game and am
trying to excel at both sports at once.)

In August, the schedule remained about the same. Nautilus twice a week, half-hour of skipping a day, four hours of
squash, but the running increased from ten to twelve miles,
still at just over a six-minute pace. In September, I stepped
up the running and skipping and took a few laps in the pool
occasionally to keep my feel for the water, but I took off
weekends because the competitive season for squash had
begun. So my Monday-through-Friday routine in September, October, November and December was as follows:
twelve miles running at a six-minute pace—I got it down to
a consistent seventy-two minutes—or the equivalent distance in intervals of miles or half-miles; one hour of skipping; two to three hours of squash; and Nautilus twice a
week. Six months of this type of work will pay off in a big
way six months later. In other words, if after forty hours of
swimming in July, I have a moment of weakness, my reserve
will not necessarily be the hard training months of May and
June; the gentle reserve background of October and November might act as the strong reserve from which I can draw.

January and February are the prime squash time, so I gave
in to the game with the confidence that the previous six
months were so intense that I could call them back at any
moment. In January and February I still ran twelve miles
five days a week; I still skipped my hour of rope; I still went

through Nautilus twice a week; and even though I didn't put
in any more hours on the squash court, I was geared toward
squash. My day revolved around getting ready for the weekend tournament. I couldn't play the best game of squash I
could play while running twelve miles a day or while skipping so much or while doing any of the heavy conditioning
workouts I do. It is a game of reflexes and alert senses.
Fatigue, mental or physical, throws your movement off;
long-distance running robs you of your quick start; the long
skipping and Nautilus, when done in direct combination
with playing, pump your muscles up, make you sluggish and
dull your racket work. But even with all of the running,
skipping and weight training, I managed to play a respectable game. However, when I swim I don't stand a prayer on
the squash court. You can't train for swimming and expect
to have quick leg speed. So I dropped the swimming altogether in January and February and added fifteen minutes
of speed bag work a day for quicker hands. The rest of the
physical day remained the same.

February 27th marked the beginning of serious training.
Except for Nautilus, I do no land training at all. Five hours
of swimming a day, every day of the week (except for the
first two weeks, which were meant to transfer my running
shape back into swimming shape). Two hours of intervals in
the morning, one hour of sprints in the midafternoon, and
two hours of straight mileage at night. April will be more of
the same, with Nautilus still twice a week and the swimming
upped from five to six to eight hours a day. I will spend the
month of April in Mission Viejo, California, where they
host the greatest swimming facility in the United States,
along with the greatest amateur swimming coach in the
United States, Mark Schubert. By the time I leave Mission

Viejo, my cardiovascular condition and strength levels will
be excellent. Then, on May 1, I will move down to Miami
with my trainer and begin two months of ocean swimming.
The first three weeks of May, I will do various workouts of
six, eight, ten and twelve hours in length. The last week in
May, I will fly down with the crew to swim around Barbados,
which is sixty miles in circumference and which will take
about twenty-four hours to circle. (I will be the first person
to swim around an entire country.) Back in Miami for the
month of June. On the first weekend, there will be a twelve-
hour swim out into the Gulf Stream with the full navigational crew and shark cage as a true test run for the Cuba
swim. The third weekend will feature another full test run
of twenty-four hours. Then I will have two weeks to taper
off and rest and fatten up. Some time during the first week
in July I will be ready, weighing in, I hope, at 140 pounds.
We will settle down in Havana and wait for the fine
weather. When the moment comes, I will stroke out of the
Havana Harbor with a competent and dedicated crew, and,
barring a hurricane or some other unforeseen disaster, I will
not leave the water until I reach the Florida Keys.

To my imagination, this swim has developed in the genre
of the old Greek myth—grandeur and excellence lie at its
core. I am truly a naiad of the sea. As Pheidippides ran the
first marathon from Marathon to Athens in 490 B.C., I shall
swim the ultimate marathon to Marathon Key.

About the Author

DIANA NYAD was born in New York City and raised in Fort Lauderdale, Florida. She began swimming when she was six months old and started training seriously at age eleven, under Olympic coach Jack Nelson. An attack of endocarditis at age sixteen and the subsequent three months in bed dashed all hopes of Olympic medals. She began training for marathon swimming in 1970. While training and swimming, Diana also attended Emory University in Atlanta, and the Université de Dijon, and graduated with honors, Phi Beta Kappa, from Lake Forest College in Lake Forest, Illinois, in 1973.

In 1973 she entered a Ph.D. program in comparative literature at New York University, and during the 1975–76 and 1976–77 school years, she coached the swimming team at Barnard College.

Diana holds the world record for men and women for a north-to-south crossing of Lake Ontario (32 miles) and the 28-mile circuit around Manhattan Island, New York. She also holds the women's world record for a 26-mile race in the Paraná River, Argentina; the 22 miles from Capri to Naples, Italy; and the 50-mile swim from the Great Barrier Reef to the Australian coast.

Diana is the second-ranked woman squash player in New York City. She gives corporate motivational seminars, speaks at youth functions and school graduations, and plays the clarinet. She has written articles for *Esquire, Quest, WomenSports, Woman* and *Mademoiselle*, and a column for *New Dawn* magazine. She lives in New York City.